Think of a Card...

Think of a Card...

by

Don Lewin OBE

With assistance from Michael Oke

Copyright (c) 2008 Don Lewin

First published in Great Britain in 2008 by Bound Biographies Limited

The right of Don Lewin to be identified as the Author of the Work has been asserted by him in accordance with the Copyright, Designs and Patent Act 1988.

A CIP catalogue record for this title is available from the British Library

ISBN 978-1-905178-23-0

Typeset in Stempel Garamond by Bound Biographies Ltd

Bound Biographies

Heyford Park House, Heyford Park

Bicester

OX25 5HD

www.boundbiographies.com

Printed and bound in the UK

To the memory of Mum and Dad
who made me what I am

| Foreword

In the time I have been putting this book together, I have had the very bad experience of falling ill with pancreatitis. I must say, for someone who has had a life of good health, this has been hard and I have taken nine months to recover. I, like so many other people, had never heard of pancreatitis – apparently, it is quite common but very little is known about it so it is not talked about. I do know, however, that it is extremely painful and that something like one in three people lose their life. I have been one of the lucky ones, and knowing now how much more is needed in this field I have decided to give all revenue earned from the sale of this book to this worthwhile cause, as well as a charity card at Christmas.

Thank you for buying this book. I hope you enjoy it.

With best wishes

Don Lewin OBE

Contents

Introduction

It had always been my ambition to own a *Rolls Royce* – that to me was the sign of having made it. However, it couldn't just be any old *Rolls Royce* (if there's such a thing), but a brand new one, and then only when it could be afforded. At the age of ten I had decided that I would only buy my dream car when I could have a brand new one... and be able to pay for it in cash. What's more, such a luxury could only be considered when the car could be parked outside my own big house.

Even as a boy it was always the strip on millionaires that I went to first in the *Sunday Pictorial*. When Dad had finished with the paper I would take it to read in bed. The weekly strip was a potted history about men who had made it from nothing, but the thing that struck me as I read week after week was that so many of these men had been given a hand up. There was a man called Nuffield, for example, who started working in a shed. He ended up as Lord Rootes, having built up the *Morris* motorcar company in Coventry. But he had been given £2,000 by his father to get started. Yes, he'd done well, but in my book that wasn't self-made... £2,000 was a considerable amount of money in 1900. Then there were *Raelbrook Toplin* shirts, 'the shirts you don't iron' as the TV ad claimed, but he had started out with 35 machinists. Some people would have been happy to end up with 35 machinists! No, my idols were those who had really made it from nothing, and I wanted to follow suit.

Don't get me wrong, I was not materialistic. It's just that I had been taught to stand on my own two feet and 20 shillings made one pound. When my friends would run to their dads and ask for a couple of bob to go to the flicks, as long as it was before the pub opened they would usually receive the money. This always surprised me because when I asked my dad for money he would tell me to go and earn it. He wasn't mean, it's just that he'd had to make his own way in life and he expected me to do the same, even as a boy.

From as early as I can remember I had one scam or other going. Be it making lead soldiers from the pipes of bombed-out houses, or doing a coke round, I invariably had a bob or two that I could call my own. But now here I was sitting in my brand new *Rolls Royce* opposite the gates of a factory ready to take my first drive in my gleaming new car.

I had waited so long for this moment and here it was. For the first time in my life I was conscious of having arrived. I felt like a goldfish in its bowl – all the workers looking at me as they poured out of the factory gates on their bicycles, having just finished the afternoon shift. I didn't feel important, just nervous that my lovely new car might get scratched. I may have looked a prize pratt as I gingerly inched along the road, but by the time I had travelled 200 miles down the motorway, had braved the horrors of the North Circular, and had made my way back to Loughton, I felt as comfortable as if I had been born in a *Roller*.

I had sold my business of seven shops, retaining just one for the sake of sentimentality as much as anything else. I had enough to live on and here I was at the age of 40, retired. But what now? I had always looked forward to the good life, but having achieved it I knew that the prospect of another 40 years with nothing to do would more than likely kill me off before the first year was through. There was nothing for it but to start again... I relished the challenge and wanted to see how far I could go.

However, before I proceed too far, I'd better take a step back and relate how it all started.

1 | An East End Boy

I was born off the Burdett Road, Bow, in the East End of London on 11ᵗʰ June 1933, the second child of John and Rose Lewin. My sister Thelma, or 'Tel' as she was known, was three years my senior; Alan came along nine years later to complete the Lewin tribe. All three of us children had modern names but I cannot vouch for the origins of mine, unless Mr Disney's duck had a greater influence than I would care to believe. I was known as Don, except by Dad who insisted on Donald, and Mum who called me Donny... well, they're the only printable names!

Tales of life in the East End are well known for their extravagant claims of hardship and woe, but I cannot confess to having had such experiences. Sure, there were families for whom times were hard, especially if the father was laid off from the docks, or perhaps never returned from the war. There were families with large numbers of children who lived on hand-me-downs and for whom the pawnbroker was a weekly saviour, but my parents had struggled to rise above that. Not only was Dad hard-working but Mum was wise – the main reason why I cannot recall ever wanting for anything. That's not to say I got all I wanted – far from it – but there was always something to eat and enough clothes... what more could a child want from life?

THINK OF A CARD...

Mum was a good cook and provided the usual fare found in the East End. For supper it was pigs' trotters, faggots or maybe stewed eels whilst listening to the radio. Saturdays meant the pie shop, pie 'n' mash 'n' liquor being the regular order. This was drowned in watered-down vinegar and to my tender taste buds tasted delicious. Even today I pop along to a local pie shop for my occasional fix of pie 'n' mash 'n' liquor.

Dad was a chimney sweep, leaving the house at 4 o'clock every morning for the start of his long day. In the winter this meant lots of small jobs – local households who had noticed the chimney smoking and wanted something done about it immediately. Dad would have to fit the work round the requirements of the family. This was not easy as the fire was the only source of power for heating, hot water and even cooking, so he had to ensure he'd finished by 2 o'clock if the lady of the house was to have any chance of cleaning up after him and getting a meal on the table at teatime. He therefore started early to get in a decent day's work, but not before the fire had had time to dampen down from the night before.

I remember my fear when I was sent up a chimney to retrieve a brush for Dad on one occasion. He covered my head with a scarf and wrapped me in sacking; I'm sure it was this experience that made me claustrophobic. I was only ten but I knew then that there must be an easier way to earn a living.

In the summer Dad did larger jobs, like cleaning and servicing boilers for factories, cinemas and churches. These places used greater forethought and the work was planned for when the weather was hot and the boilers not in use. Most families did not plan in advance like this because money was tight and the chimney would only be swept when needed. Also, most people rented their homes so there was no guarantee that if they had their chimney swept in July they would still be living there the following November, sometimes a moonlight flit being necessary to keep one step ahead of the landlord. My dad responded to this way of life and was always up for the 'rush job'. He was certainly not frightened of hard work – something which was instilled into me from an early age.

When Dad got home from work in the early afternoon his first job was to store the bags of soot in the yard, because when he had enough he sold them to a firm in Bedford who dealt in fertiliser. As he was filthy, he would then strip to the waist and have a good wash, throwing handfuls of soda into the water. For him, as with most people, having a bath was a weekly event in front of the fire when we children had gone to bed.

When Dad came indoors he would take all the coins from his pocket and wash them to get rid of the soot. He then placed the money on the mantelpiece for Mum – this was the system they operated, share and share alike.

Being a hard-working and enterprising man, Dad's working day did not stop there. As he had most of the afternoon and early evening still ahead of him, and in an effort to get on in life, he always had some other venture in the pipeline.

We lived in a two-bedroom flat above a garage, at the back of which was a small factory which sold and stored bulbs. There were also several lock-ups and Dad rented these to small businesses. There was a fishmonger's, which stank, especially in the summer. Another chap imported bananas which, ordinarily, were not easy to come by. However, as we used to nick some I never appreciated quite what a luxury they really were. Another small company made pith helmets for the Royal Marines, and there was also the blacksmith who I loved to watch going about his work. Not only did the renting of these lock-ups bring Dad a bit of extra income, but it also gave him the space to dabble in his own ventures.

A few of the lock-ups were rented by some of Dad's friends for their motorbikes. Dad also loved these and always had a motorbike and sidecar. He used a couple of the lock-ups to build bicycles from old bike parts in the afternoons after he had finished sweeping chimneys. He made a few bob this way and soon progressed to buying and selling cars, often going to the local car auctions to see what he could find. He kept some of these cars, renting them out as self-drive to generate cash.

My father was not backwards in coming forward when it came to making money and he would not pass up on any opportunity. If we were on Dad's motorbike and drew up next to a car at traffic lights, he would often gesture to the driver to wind down the window and then ask, "Is this the car that's for sale?" On one or two occasions this direct approach resulted in us pulling over to the roadside and Dad doing the deal there and then.

On another occasion, after the war, I was with Dad when we pulled up at a garage to get some petrol. While the attendant was filling up the car Dad nosed around in his usual fashion. Spying a large car sheeted up at the back of the lot he proceeded to make further enquiries. It turned out that it was a *Daimler* which had previously belonged to the chairman of *Austin Reed*. After the war rationing was as strict as it had been during hostilities, in some cases more so. Industry was still a long way from getting back on its feet and many goods, cars included, were in short supply. Indeed, new vehicles were at such a premium that it was illegal to sell a brand new one within a year of it being purchased. Second-hand cars could command two or three times the price of a brand new one and the government was keen to prevent a black market trade. This *Daimler* was not new but it was a car, and a posh one at that and Dad wanted it. He used his pay-off money from the Army, plus a few reserves he had built up from his other wheeling and dealing activities, becoming the proud owner of this luxury car. However, the car was not for his own use – certainly not when there was money to be made. Dad cashed in on his day job by setting up a business called *Lucky Sweep's Car Hire*. He rented out the *Daimler* for weddings and funerals, often joining forces with two or three other contacts he had if a fleet of cars was required.

There were many wide boys in the East End, but coupled with Dad's eye for a bargain was Mum's wisdom and support, which made a potent combination. We tend to take our parents for granted, but looking back now I suppose that their qualities were my training ground for things to come. However, at the time, as a boy on the streets of the Mile End Road, I felt that my family was just the same as the rest... except that perhaps we paid our rent on time.

I admired Mum and Dad for their independence. They had many friends, but my parents stood out from most of our neighbours because they did not smoke or drink and chose not to spend their evenings in the pub. They did not make an issue of this, but I think it was probably a reaction to their parents' over-fondness of the stuff. Certainly Mum's father was not the sort of man you would have wanted to pick an argument with, and I think that Dad resented the money his parents wasted on fags and booze. Whether it was a conscious decision that they wanted to better themselves I cannot say, but they had a very strong work ethic and a desire to make their way in life.

My paternal grandfather, Fred Hood, worked on a brewer's dray for *Mann and Crossmann* and so I suppose a liking for ale was an occupational hazard. His hobby was keeping pigeons, but I still found it odd when this brute of a man later moved with his family to the countrified new town of Dagenham to take up more genteel delights. I wonder what his former drinking pals would have thought of this ex-Army type with a fish pond and aviary!

We lived opposite *The Lord Raglan* pub and Tel and I took great delight in watching the antics at throwing-out time. The pattern was invariably the same: it started off congenially enough with a sing-song, usually the likes of *Nellie Dean*, but then a word would be spoken out of turn or perhaps be taken the wrong way and a drunken brawl would ensue. However, just as quickly as it had turned nasty it would all change again and become amicable, the men professing undying love for each other. Tel and I thought it was all great fun... as long as Mum and Dad didn't catch us out of bed at the window.

As my parents didn't frequent the pub they had the time and money to spend their evenings in other pursuits. The most exciting of these was going to speedway meetings, usually at West Ham on a Tuesday, although we also went to New Cross and Wembley from time to time. Dad was a real fanatic and that enthusiasm was soon shared by me, my idol being Lionel Van Prague. Speedway was for all the family and Mum and Tel would come too. We would all travel on the motorbike, Mum on the back behind Dad, and me and Tel in the sidecar... it always seemed so unfair that she got the front with the big seat and all the leg room while I was squeezed in behind her.

Another great passion was the cinema and it was not unusual for us to go three times a week. There were plenty of places to choose from, but our most regular haunts were the *Empire* in Stepney, the *Troxy* in Commercial Road and the *Odeon* in the Mile End Road.

I also went to the flicks with the other lads on a regular basis, but not all these excursions met with success. Our usual mode of entrance was via the side fire doors with the aid of a wire coat hanger to release the bar from the outside. These doors were in a covered alcove and one day, on hearing a noise above and venturing out, we were met by a torrent of water poured from above by the vigilant projectionist on his tea-break. Whilst this was a disappointing end to our intended afternoon in front of the big screen, a greater dilemma now faced us: how to get dry before our mums saw our clothes, because inevitably that would have ended with a belting. Such were the worries of a schoolboy in wartime London.

Many of the locals went 'hopping' in the hop fields of Kent for a holiday. From what I understand, this usually involved working dog hard during the day followed by bouts of heavy drinking at night... pretty much the same as usual for most of the dockers. I'm not sure if it was that which did not appeal to my parents, or perhaps because we could afford something a little better, but we usually went camping to Dymchurch. We stayed on a site at the back of *The Old Ship Hotel* which had tents already pitched. This was just as well as we couldn't take much with us, travelling as we did on the trusty old motorbike and sidecar.

We would do all the usual things at the seaside, but the annual ritual was a ride on the Dymchurch to Hythe steam railway. The holiday sped by all too quickly, not least because we never went for a week; it was normally just a long weekend as Dad would need to get back to work.

However, we also had 'days out', which usually meant going to Southend. This was a great treat, not least because Southend had the *Kurzal*, a massive funfair with everything a boy could wish for, especially the 'Wall of Death'! It was always the highlight of my day to marvel at these brave motorcyclists riding horizontal to the ground, and I would dream that one day I too would be able to have the chance. I can still capture that sense of excitement, the noise, the anticipation, the fear, the exhaust fumes – wonderful. The perfect conclusion to the day was to have a 'topper upper'. This was a *Rossi's* ice cream with not just one scoop, but two... we knew how to live!

As I had no older brothers I always had clothes of my own, although Dad would ensure they were a couple of sizes too big so there was room for growth. I vowed that one day I would be able to afford clothes that fitted me.

Once in a while Dad would take me to *Wickhams*, a big store in the Mile End Road, to get a coat perhaps, or maybe some boots. However, new boots were few and far between as running repairs were the order of the day – usually another row of 'blakeys'. I would ask Dad, "When can I wear shoes?" His answer was always the same, "When you stop being a street-raker."

I remember feeling proud the first day I wore long (very long!) trousers; I had to dress smartly as I was going to see Gran. My mother sent me to get my hair cut, and whilst waiting I stood in front of the fire. The barber smelt burning and I could feel my trousers getting hot... when I touched the backs of my legs the material was scorched and just disintegrated in my fingers. I went home terrified of Mum's reaction. Needless to say, it was a long time before I wore long trousers again.

Common sights on the streets were the tallyman, the insurance man, the 'School Board', the coalman, rag and bone, *Carter Paterson* and the 'stop me and buy one' trike... my favourite being a *Shale's* lemon ice. Another regular was the brewer's dray pulled by the Shire horses, but this resulted in a sore bottom for me when Dad found me climbing on the back of the wagon one too many times. I felt it was unfair that Dad took his belt off to me whereas Tel always seemed to be able to wrap him round her little finger. When Alan came along, he too seemed to get away with murder – such are the trials of being an older son.

I was not immune to such victimisation at school either and often got the cane for some misdemeanour or other, usually for being late. However, my tardy timekeeping was not without its rewards because Mum gave me sixpence for doing the dishes throughout the week, so if we were late for breakfast I had the option of no money or a sore hand... no contest.

I was not aware of the importance of the war or of any of its major milestones. All I knew was that a horrible man called Hitler was bad, we were good and that we would win. The war was something I did not question, perhaps like being born a boy and not a girl. Much of the time it was very ordinary and things like shortages and air raids meant nothing special as I knew no different.

THINK OF A CARD...

Like any child I was only interested in those things which affected me and my family.

On the day war broke out I can remember that people were very sad and that as soon as the siren went all the streets emptied. We didn't have an air raid shelter at this time and so went to the basement of *The Lord Raglan* along with several other families. They sang songs, the only one of which I can remember was *Land of Hope and Glory*.

Many children had been sent away to live with strangers in other parts of the country. That didn't sound like much fun and I was glad that I had not been 'evacuated'. What's more, there didn't seem much point in going away because nothing dangerous seemed to be happening. Sure, strange things started to appear in the sky – huge great balloons covered with dozens of wires. I was to learn that they were barrage balloons and the cables were meant to bring down enemy planes, or at least stop them from flying too low to bomb us accurately... but I never saw any planes at this time.

All the metal railings were taken away to melt down and use for the war effort, and thousands of sandbags were filled and placed everywhere – hospitals, police stations, underground stations etc. What struck me as odd was that they were called sandbags yet they were filled with earth... grown-ups could be strange!

We often sat in the basement of *The Lord Raglan* while the adults played cards, but nothing exciting happened. Later we had our own Morrison shelter, an iron table which we had to sleep under, but the novelty of this soon wore off. We also had to carry gas masks everywhere and they smelled horrid when we had to put them on. We had gas drills at school.

An ugly incident remains vivid in my memory – the emergence of the Blackshirts, as Oswald Moseley's fascist movement was known. These meetings were just a curiosity to a nipper, but I became aware of the Blackshirts being far more sinister when, in broad daylight, they beat up Mr Kirsch, a Jewish barber. I couldn't understand why they would want to hurt this nice man, especially as it meant that he left the area shortly afterwards.

After a while some of the children who had been evacuated came home, the rest of us having gone back to our usual way of life because nothing was happening. Then, in September 1940, a year after the outbreak of war, things changed dramatically. German bombers attacked Woolwich Arsenal and at the end of the month the nightly raids began. From then on bombing, fires, smoke and devastation became a way of life. We used to go out the following day and collect shrapnel from the streets.

I found that war could be exciting, like the time when I watched a dogfight with Uncle George and saw a German bail out. His parachute landed only a few streets away and the neighbours went after him wielding shovels. Other times were awful, especially feeling frightened of the noise and fire and seeing Mum crying.

Shortly after this Tel and I were evacuated to stay with a family called Perrin in Hertfordshire. They were friends of Uncle Bill, and Mum told us to be brave as this would only be for a short time until she could find a place where we could all be together. True to her word, four or five months later she collected us and took us to the neighbouring village of Braughing, Dad by this time being in the RAF. Mum had found a small cottage to rent, which became our home for the next two years.

THINK OF A CARD...

The sleepy Hertfordshire villages were quite a shock to us, being such a contrast with London. I remember seeing my first ever kingfisher and being mesmerised by the amazing colours. I also loved the pig farm, often helping out... I had never seen a pig before!

Other children had been evacuated to these parts and I soon made many friends at the village school, both with other evacuees and with some of the local children. I discovered a whole new world of adventure, playing in the woods and fields, but my favourite was playing by the River Lea and, in the summer, skinny dipping. I also loved all the wildlife, particularly the water rats and otters.

I soon found myself working to make some money. The big house at the end of the village looked good for a few bob. I started by cleaning their rabbit hutch, for which I earned sixpence a week, and once I had gained their confidence I was able to move onto larger jobs. Having a huge garden as they did there were always plenty of chores to be done and I soon became an invaluable and well rewarded asset to their lives. Once my work was out of the way I was able to play in the garden, and also in their big toy room, as I went to school with the children who lived there.

There were cherry trees in the garden, delicacies which were new to me... but I ate my fill to make up for any lost time. Similarly I had never seen apple trees or gooseberry bushes before and these fruits also became a regular part of my diet. Cobnuts collected from the hedgerows were tasty, and blackberrying was also fun, although I seem to remember that this had more to do with the fact that Violet was there – at the grand old age of nine I was having my first crush.

We ate bantam eggs in Braughing, whatever a bantam was! I looked after the hens for Mrs Page and fed them with mash she made up from potato peelings. We grew some of our own vegetables, and many of the neighbours were very generous in offering us some of theirs. We ate very well and I even tasted duck for the first time, but I still hankered after pie 'n' mash 'n' liquor.

This may all sound idyllic, but there were disadvantages to living in the back of beyond. For a start, we now had to go outside to attend to calls of nature. There was a block of toilets at the back of our row of cottages, each cubicle consisting of a wooden bench with a hole, beneath which stood a large bucket. Carbolic in the bucket did little to alleviate the horrendous stench. Men came round twice a week to empty these buckets – and no, this was not a job for which I would volunteer, however much money was on offer! The chap next-door, Mr Cook, used to empty his own bucket... on the rhubarb. It was strange how I never felt hungry whenever his rhubarb was being offered around.

There was no running water, all our needs being met by the village pump. We therefore had to be very careful about the water we used, and whenever we had a bath there was barely enough to drown a mouse. This made skinny dipping in the river all the more attractive.

There was a wash house next to the block of toilets behind the cottages. Each household had its own boiler, which was a big iron cauldron under which a fire had to be built and lit. On Mondays it was a real hive of activity, collecting water from the pump to fill the boiler, and my services were in much demand. If it was raining the process was more difficult, but at least the water butts near the wash house were filled, reducing the number of trips to the village pump.

THINK OF A CARD...

We had been used to gas and electric in London, but no such luxuries were available in Braughing. Mum cooked on a range heated by an open fire, and we used oil lamps for illumination and candles when we went to bed. It felt as if we were in a time warp.

There was a village shop, but this only provided a few necessities, so on Saturday Tel and I would go with Mum to either Bishop's Stortford or Hertford if we needed anything extra. We liked going to these towns as they both had a cinema and Mum would take us along if we'd been good... well, reasonably good.

Dad came and saw us on the few occasions he had leave owing to him and it was good to be back as a real family again, even if it was in unusual surroundings. Our family was soon to increase because in 1942 we were joined by Alan who was born in Hertford Hospital. Sensing that her time was near, Mum made her way to Hertford, but when she got there the delivery was not as imminent as she had suspected so she went to the cinema to see Dorothy Lamour in *Aloma of the South Seas*. I don't know if it was anything to do with the high drama of the film, but when she came out of the cinema she went to the hospital next-door where Alan was promptly born.

By 1943 Mum felt that things had quietened down sufficiently in London for us to return. This may have been a little premature because in June 1944 Hitler sent us a present, his reprisal weapon, the V1, or 'doodlebug' as it became known. This was a pilotless aircraft packed with high explosives and when the engine cut out the doodlebug fell to earth with devastating consequences. The first time we saw one we mistook it for a plane on fire – it crashed in Grove Road. We never made that mistake again.

My schooling had been totally disrupted because of the war, not just from evacuation. In the early part of the war I had often been too tired to work, having spent the night under the Morrison shelter. Now the doodlebugs created even more havoc, with schools again closing because of bomb damage or a lack of teachers.

Two of the schools I attended were closed thanks to Herr Hitler, one of them being totally flattened. However, I must admit that this did not cause me undue worry; at best, school had been a necessary evil, and as it was usually several weeks, or even months, before new accommodation could be found or made fit for our schooling, I was quite happy to put my free hours to good use.

I was now becoming quite used to the destruction of war and could see that bombed-out houses provided plenty of opportunities to make a bob or two. One venture was to collect old bits of timber to chop up for firewood. It was better if I could lay my hands on some of the larger pieces, but as these were needed for rebuilding work I had to be careful in my scavenging. At two bob a sack the wood was quite a nice little earner and there were always plenty of buyers. I soon built up a round of regulars and delivered the sacks to the door in a borrowed wheelbarrow. On Saturday mornings a couple of friends and I delivered coke from the gasworks, having collected orders and the money the previous evening.

The father of a friend of mine was even more advanced in his thinking and by recruiting three of us schoolboys he ran a lucrative sideline. Firstly we would collect any old fragments of lead piping we could find; this was usually no problem the morning after a visit by the Luftwaffe. We would struggle with what we could to Bert's dad's house and melt the lead in a big old saucepan on the stove.

THINK OF A CARD...

Somehow Mr Jenkins had managed to come by some moulds for toy soldiers and we filled these with the molten lead. Once cooled, the mould was removed and with a bit of tidying up the resultant soldier was quite respectable to all but the expert eyes of a drill sergeant.

The models were then ready for painting, which we undertook in the evenings on piecework. Bill Jenkins was an enterprising chap because by paying us in this way we never knew quite how much he was making... but you can be sure it was worth his while.

The final part of the business was for Bill to load us up with these lead soldiers in stout canvas bags and send us off to various markets. My patch was at the end of the Mile End market opposite Toynbee Hall. I would lay out some sacking and set up my wares. I never had a legitimate stall, but I suppose Bill worked on the principle that the Old Bill would turn a blind eye to a young lad like me looking to make a few bob.

This was my first experience of being paid commission and I realised that I was quite good at selling. Knowing that I could make money for each soldier I sold soon removed any lingering inhibitions I may have had. I also quickly latched on to the concept of reducing the price for a bulk order as it was worth forsaking a couple of coppers if I could sell half-a-dozen soldiers at a time. I was also happy to take orders for different coloured uniforms as this would ensure repeat sales. Bill was obviously quite pleased with me because I found that my canvas bag got heavier and heavier... it certainly helped to build up my muscles.

Back at a newly patched up St Paul's School, I saw a doodlebug flashing past the open space of what had been a window. However, the engine didn't cut out, but just screamed straight into its target giving us no time to hide under the desks. It landed very close to the school and we huddled together as best we could as the ceiling caved in. Once the dust had settled and we had established that no one was injured, a few of the older boys passed round the bottles of milk to help clear our throats. Everybody was covered in dust and dirt, and we started to laugh at each other's black faces.

The fear uppermost in my mind was for Mum and Alan. We lived close to the school and the doodlebug couldn't have landed far away. I slipped out of the classroom, as did a couple of other lads clearly with the same thought in their minds. The teacher chased after us, but he had no chance of catching us and we were soon over the wall at the back of the playground and off in different directions.

Many houses had been damaged and I was in a state of panic. I clambered over the rubble without any regard to the precarious structures and crashing masonry; in any case I could barely see ten yards ahead because of all the dust and smoke. As I neared the end of the road I saw a few houses still reasonably intact, and thankfully ours was among them. I ran through the void where the front door had stood, looking for signs of life. Amid the dust and devastation I heard a sound so familiar, but which this time I was so delighted to hear... Alan crying. He was under the Morrison shelter with Mum who was hugging him for all she was worth. They were both unscathed.

By this time Bill Jenkins had progressed to a legitimate pitch in Club Row market. He sold anything and everything and I often helped out. I remember that a particularly easy line to sell was when he bred dogs and put the pups on the stall. It was perfect – people would almost always stop to look, often asking to hold one. Once the cute little puppy was in their arms, it was as good as sold. Bill would write out pedigree certificates the night before to get a better price. I really enjoyed Sunday mornings in the Club Row dog market.

School leaving age was 14, but in my final year that was increased to 15, much to my annoyance. This coincided with our move to Wanstead, so on my first day at Aldersbrook School I wore my best suit. It was double-breasted with a wide, grey, chalk pinstripe, rounded off with a Windsor knotted tie as preferred by spivs and considered smart apparel for the East End of London. I looked the business... or so I thought. As I entered the classroom, all eyes turned towards the new boy. Everyone wore posh blazers and grey trousers or skirts. I didn't even know there was a school uniform and I felt like a circus clown.

It was never pleasant going to a new school, not least because there were all the usual initiation rites to go through. I remember looking round the class to see who was the biggest and therefore who I would have to fight first. In my East End schools, you were only ever accepted after at least a couple of bleeding noses – preferably not your own. However, at Aldersbrook no one made any threatening approaches towards me, which, rather than making me feel accepted, left me with the peculiar sensation of not being wanted... I wasn't even worthy of being beaten up!

Mr Gough was the headmaster and he taught the top class. His area of expertise was Art, but he provided a solid education in all the basic subjects. I don't know if he saw me as his special assignment, but he seemed to take me under his wing and I am grateful for his patience.

I chewed gum all the time, which did not meet with Mr Gough's approval. However, rather than reprimanding me he used humour. He called me 'Betsy' and was frequently heard to say, in response to some request by me, "OK Betsy, empty your mouth and let's start again."

I was significantly behind the others in the class with my education. In an effort to help me catch up Mr Gough provided lessons after school and I did my best to thank him by being conscientious in my studies. I learned more in this one year with Mr Gough than I did in all my previous years of schooling combined.

There was one subject in which I was not behind and I saw this as a great chance to prove my worth. French was not taught until the final year and so we all started from scratch. At Prize Giving at the end of that year I won the award for French, along with the comment, "Lewin, we all find it difficult to see how you can do so well in French when you are still having so many problems speaking English!" They never did get used to my cockney accent.

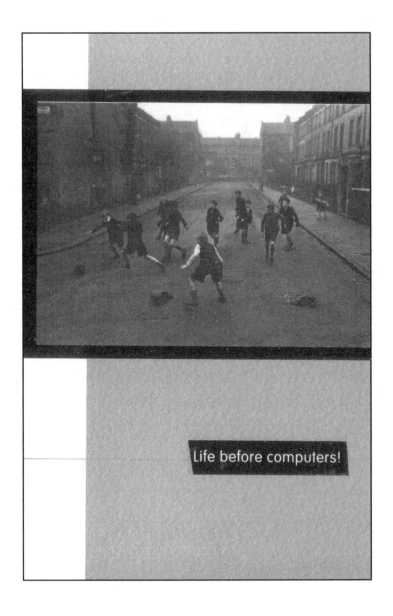

Life before computers!

2 | Growing Up

When I left school I had the romantic notion of being a press photographer – not that I was exactly qualified for the task as I'd only used a borrowed Box Brownie on a handful of occasions. I suppose I was attracted by the glamour and excitement of the job, reporting on murders, top sporting events and rubbing shoulders with the rich and famous. So keen was I on this career that I traipsed up and down Fleet Street knocking on the doors of the big newspaper offices. However, as soon as I was asked about my background and qualifications I was always met with the same negative response. Naïve I may have been, but I cannot be accused of being unambitious.

The reality was far different to the fantasy and instead of mixing with celebrities I found myself mixing concrete. I got a job as a labourer with a firm of high class builders, *Hicks & Son*, and for the next three years turned my hand to just about everything. It seemed that for months on end my sole function in life was to fetch and carry anything... as long as it was very heavy. My only respite was to make copious cups of tea – there was no coffee in those days for the likes of us.

My boss, Jack Hicks, was a master craftsman whose area of expertise was hanging wallpaper. Initially I thought this was easy, but once I'd seen the way to do it properly I appreciated the art involved. Mr Hicks gathered similar artisans around him, painters, grainers, carpenters, bricklayers and the like, all of which was quite admirable given the prevailing conditions. London was emerging from a period of utter devastation. I doubt if there was a road for miles around which had avoided at least some damage and there were just not enough builders to go round. This led to a huge increase in cowboy builders, most people being only too delighted to see a workman turn up with his bag of tools. It was only a matter of days later, in some cases a few hours, before the unlucky mugs realised the error of their ways and had to look for a decent builder.

Hicks & Son operated at the quality end of the market, refusing to compromise standards just because of increased demand. I learned a considerable amount working with such craftsmen and soon realised that I would have a long apprenticeship ahead of me if I chose a career in this industry. I seemed to have a knack for dealing with basic pipework, but I also enjoyed doing many other jobs once I'd got through the phase of being tea-boy. All this gave me a confidence and willingness to give anything a go. However, even more important was what it instilled regarding quality. It might cost a little more, but quality wins the day every time.

I wasn't frightened of hard work, and the benefit of being prepared to help out with anything meant that I started to earn more. Initially I was on 38 shillings (£1.90) a week, but by the time I was called up for National Service three years later, this had risen to the dizzy heights of £9. When I started work I had given Mum half my wages for board and keep and I continued this right up until

I went into the Army. I was pleased to thank Mum in this way, especially as I always had enough for my moderate lifestyle.

There were some lighter moments when working for *Hicks & Son* as I was always known as a bit of a live-wire. One time some of us were painting a house in Wanstead. As it was near 5th November there were fireworks in abundance and I had one of those Thunder Flashes or 'bombs' as they were called. I waited for one of the guys to get settled in the outside toilet and then calmly rolled the Thunder Flash under the door so it would stop at his feet. The noise in such a confined space was unbelievable and he came rushing out with his trousers round his knees, as mad as a bull! I'm not sure if he kicked the door open or if it was the force of the explosion, but either way he chased me for at least a mile. I had picked the wrong bloke; he was an ex-guardsman, but I was glad I was much younger and faster. Needless to say, I never went back to work that day.

I was at the flicks one day with my mates when we got chatting to some girls. I got on particularly well with one and left my mates to go and sit with her – sorry boys, all's fair in love and war! However, they had the last laugh as this 'date' was not destined to last. All was going well until I tried to impress her by producing an orange I'd smuggled into the cinema. Oranges were difficult to come by, so she was suitably impressed. She was less impressed when I tried to peel it. I jammed my thumb into the peel, the juice squirted up into her eye, so Amen to that date!

My next real learning exercise was in the Army and boy, did I have a lot to learn. I began my National Service in August 1951 and was sent directly to the transit camp at Aldershot where I spent four weeks being kitted out and receiving basic training. I soon discovered this was where they separated the wheat from the chaff. The wheat went off for officer training, whilst the chaff remained... I remained.

We were preached at regarding the merits and honour of belonging to the King's Army and how therefore it would be assumed that we would all want to sign on for at least three years. Few of us felt an overwhelming desire to concur, which did not endear us to our lords and masters. The way we looked at it, there were countless disadvantages yet only two small advantages of signing on for a commission: one was a slightly increased rate of pay and the second was that we would be more likely to receive a favourable posting. For example, I quite fancied the prospect of being a dog handler in Malaysia, but I was told that this would only be open to me if I served for at least another year – I like dogs, but not that much.

Most of the lads moaned about the ill-fitting uniform, but we soon got them into shape and I had no complaints. Then there were the injections. The pain of a blunt needle being jabbed into my arm is one thing, but what I found more disconcerting was the colour of the cotton wool swab. It was black when it got to me – so much for medical hygiene.

Everyone who has done National Service has his own story of injustice, and I'm no exception. My particular gripe at the transit camp relates to having my hair cut. Like most of the others I had been to the barber a few days before arriving in Aldershot in a vain attempt to avoid the attentions of the camp barber. I should have known it would be to no avail because however short our hair was, and for some of the chaps this was pretty short, we all had to wait our turn to be dehumanised. I was shorn along with everyone else and accepted the fact that I was unlikely to win a beauty contest for the foreseeable future.

The next day on parade my hair was not considered short enough and I was told to get it cut again. Even though I was aware of the randomness of being singled out in this fashion, having heard similar versions of this particular stunt before joining up, it still didn't make the experience any easier to take. I duly traipsed off back to the barber, meeting chaps from other units who had been made similar stooges. We all agreed that our hair was no longer than anyone else in our unit and took solace from the fact that their turn would come. As far as I was concerned, I left the camp barber's with as much hair as I had when I entered, but at least I'd complied with orders.

The following day on parade I made an extra special effort to ensure that there was nothing untoward about my appearance. Surely it now had to be someone else's turn. How wrong I was. Within minutes I found myself in the barber's chair again... for the third time in as many days.

Whilst my experience was perhaps a little more farcical than most, the very process of ensuring that we had virtually no hair on our heads served the purposes of the Army well. We were not allowed off base during our basic training, and having barnets like ours made it an easy job for the MPs to spot any likely miscreants. The humiliation also served another purpose. As far as the powers-that-be were concerned, it was essential that any spark of initiative be squeezed from us. A unit of men must think as one and act as one, and anyone with original ideas must be crushed. Any Jack-the-lads soon found themselves engaged in various mind-numbing

29

pursuits like digging the grass with a knife and fork or perhaps cleaning the toilets with a toothbrush... the Army always won.

I found this out for myself when I had a run-in with Corporal Bates. I should have known better because he had done his time and was leaving that week. I didn't like the way he was throwing his weight around with a couple of the lads, twins who wouldn't say boo to a goose. When I felt he had gone too far, I piped up with, "It's alright for you... if you didn't have those stripes on your arm you wouldn't pick on them." He immediately took his jacket off and came at me. Whilst we were trying to wrestle each other to the ground an officer walked in. Obviously I was the one deemed to be in the wrong and I found myself on a charge – not a good start to my Army life. After only three days I discovered the joys of polishing the guardroom floor with a 'bumper' – a horrendously heavy contraption with a mind of its own – until the floor shone and you could see your face in it.

Transit camp was a strange experience as most of us were not much more than boys playing at being adults. Hearing sobs from the other beds was not an uncommon sound those first few nights, few of us ever having left home before. I adapted well to being away from my family, but not so some of the men. The communal showers were another telling phase. It was easy to spot those who had never been involved in team games... they were the ones creeping round holding their towels for dear life.

I was posted to Portsmouth for my initial training, being lumped in with a couple of dozen other chaps. We were not a very promising bunch; because of the wartime upheaval to our education, some of the lads could not even read. However, this did not seem to cause any problems – our drill sergeant only wanted us to put one foot in front of the other, not write an essay about it.

After we had been in Portsmouth a few days and had spoken to some of the seasoned veterans – chaps who were all of a month ahead of us – we appreciated that our drill sergeant was a pretty good chap. Sure, he had to shout at a ridiculous volume and go through the motions of being a b******d, but as long as we did our best and did not give him a hard time, he was fair to us, and from the stories we heard about some of the other drill sergeants, that was a blessing indeed.

If I was to write a book about National Service, the cookhouse would warrant a chapter of its own. It was a hub of social activity and usually a pleasant place to be, assuming you were not on fatigues of one form or another: spud bashing, pot washing etc. However, the relative informality of the cookhouse meant that it was easy to let your guard slip, and if you did you soon realised the error of your ways. The same rules applied here as elsewhere, keep your head down, play the game and don't get too big for your boots. You would be adequately fed and watered, although any highly sensitive taste buds would not be overly challenged. That having been said, because the food tray was used for both main course and dessert, with only shallow hollows for each, it did result in some interesting combinations – the mixture of watery gravy and thin custard became quite a speciality.

The golden rule was not to take liberties and when asked a question give the required answer. Drill sergeants were not paid to think on their feet; unless they received the response they were expecting they would sound off at you, no matter how well you thought you knew them. I obviously still had a lot to learn because I felt that our drill sergeant was a decent bloke and could take a gentle amount of cheek... wrong.

My mistake came when he was regimental sergeant for the day and was doing the usual rounds in the cookhouse. He walked between the tables checking that everything was alright, and even though it rarely was – the food was too cold, tasteless etc – he needed to hear the words "Yes, Sergeant." I thought that my reply of, "Yes Sergeant..." then muttering under my breath, "... but I could do with a bit more though," was well judged, showing my pals that I was on good terms with him, yet not being too familiar.

I knew I had overstepped the mark as soon as he stopped in his tracks and glared at me. The hall went silent and I became the focus of dozens of pairs of eyes. I could feel the blood rushing to my face as the regimental sergeant barked at the orderly officer to come over, whereupon he rephrased my complaint for all to hear. "This soldier here would like some more food." Oliver Twist was then marched at the double to the front of the queue whereupon a huge dollop of 'pom' was heaped onto my mess tin. I then had to stand there whilst I made my way through it, without showing any signs of being unappreciative towards my compassionate benefactor. This was not easy because pom, dehydrated mashed potato, was pretty tasteless at the best of times. It was easier to digest when awash with brown and yellow gravy-cum-custard, but I had no such luxury. It was even less easy to eat when burning with embarrassment and knowing that I had very little time to consume my seconds as we were due out on parade imminently. I didn't feel quite so clever when I left the cookhouse that day.

Thankfully the rest of my time was less eventful. I found the square bashing to be as tolerable as it can be and just went along with the games played at kit inspection. Everything was based on cleanliness and uniformity, but one of the chaps in our unit had other ideas. On a routine kit inspection fleas were found on his pillow, and when he was ordered to open his locker it was infested. Unbeknown to the rest of us he had not been washing his kit and his socks were crawling with these mites. He was treated to a regimental bath and then sent to the barber... the results of which made me appreciate that my hairstyle in Aldershot, despite three sittings, was not as severe as it might have been.

I had learned the error of my ways from the cookhouse incident and kept my head down for the rest of my time at drill camp. Thankfully the sergeant was not a man to bear grudges as he recommended me as 'Stick Man' at the passing-out parade. Now, for the first time in weeks we were allowed out of camp... the beer certainly tasted good that night. However, before being let loose on the good folk of Portsmouth we were all shown the proverbial film on VD and other sexually transmitted diseases. Boy! They frightened the hell out of you!

A couple of nights later I was offered a ticket to a dance. This particular dance hall had been declared out of bounds to Army personnel, but in true military fashion, as soon as anything was made illegal it became all the more sought after. However, my time at the dance was short-lived because the minute we went through the door into the dance hall one of my mates had a bottle thrown in his face by a local thug. As he was standing there bleeding, I argued with the bouncers, trying to get our money back as I had just paid for us to get in. I was given short shrift, which was very frustrating. The rest of the evening was spent in the emergency department of the local hospital while my mate had his face stitched up. I suppose the Army did sometimes have a reason for their rulings!

I must have been almost unrecognisable to my parents when I went on my first 48-hour leave. However, even if I had joined a man's world, I was still Dad's son, and he made sure I knew it. When I asked if he could lend me a couple of quid for my fare back to camp, he gave it to me without hesitation but suggested that if I could not afford to come home then not to bother. I was very upset by this and told him I'd never ask him for money again. Mum wrote to me later and apologised for Dad's strange way of thinking. I knew Dad wasn't mean. It was his way of making me stand on my own two feet, and looking back I know he was right.

Next came the lottery of learning what was in store for us for the remainder of our National Service. I quite fancied the idea of being a guardsman, but they had other ideas. Chaps were being posted all over the world, with favourite destinations being Korea, Malaya, Cyprus, Germany and Israel. I liked the sound of Cyprus, which was relatively trouble-free at the time, but my main hope was to avoid one of the dangerous places. Whilst I am as patriotic as the next man, probably more so, I had survived the war and certainly did not want to be a hero just for National Service.

I was drafted to the unit destined for Egypt, a place about which I knew little. However, a short while before I was kitted out I received a message telling me to report to the orderly room at the double as there was a telephone call for me. This had to be something serious. It was Ron Saunders on the phone – he was my brother-in-law, having married Tel a few months earlier. It transpired that my mother was very ill in hospital and that I should return immediately. Before I was granted compassionate leave I had to wait for a couple of hours whilst the orderly checked the facts with the police station closest to home, as it was not unknown for such stories to be fabricated in order to gain leave.

Those two hours seemed like an eternity waiting for that telephone to ring, and all the while I was haunted by my thoughts... what was wrong with Mum? How had she gone downhill so quickly? I had only seen her a few weeks before and she seemed fine... surely she would live... she must... would I ever see her alive again?

Finally the call came through from Whitechapel Police Station confirming Ron's message and I was rushed by jeep to the station to catch the last train back to London that night. When I arrived at the hospital I was met by Dad, Tel, Ron and Alan and by their faces I could tell that my worries had not been without foundation. I had to wait before I could go in to see Mum. She was in an oxygen tent, not even aware of my presence. She never came round and died three hours later. I was devastated. My mum was gone... she was only 41.

I was given two weeks' compassionate leave to attend to various bits and pieces and for the funeral. Upon my return to Portsmouth I arrived at 2.00 am and went straight to my old billet. Another unit was there and someone was sleeping in what had been my bed, not that it mattered as I was in no mood for sleep. I just stood at the window looking out into the night... I felt lonelier then than at any other time in my life, before or since.

THINK OF A CARD...

I had missed the draft to Egypt and was told that I would now be joining a tank corps being posted to the British Army on the Rhine (BAOR). Initially I was sent to Didcot for a two-month course, but during this time my posting fell through, so I was eventually sent to join a tank corps in Cambridge, a depot for tanks unfit for action. It was our job to service what we could and preserve the rest. In my experience we only ever seemed to move the tanks from one place to another and then back again.

The job might sound tedious, but for the first few months it was quite interesting getting to know about tanks, and at least we were far away from any danger zones. That's not to say that the posting was without incident. One poor chap had his hand in the wrong place when a breach block unexpectedly slipped. He was rushed off to hospital, but there was nothing they could do without the fingers. By the time we got his fingers out of the machinery the ambulance had already left – we put them in a jar and rushed them to the hospital, but it was too late for anything to be done with them.

My unit was based at Royston, but towards the end of 1952 we had to move out to make room for the 'Z Men' (reservists) who were called back to deal with a potential problem in Korea. Consequently, we were transferred to another camp which consisted of some pretty grim wartime Nissen huts. The camp was overrun with rats and the toilet facilities were horrendous. Each block of three toilets was divided only by a piece of sacking hung from the ceiling. It was very embarrassing... but at least we could swap comics.

I remember being in jankers for some minor misdemeanour or other and was told to report to the sergeant in the cookhouse for further instruction. One of the jobs he gave me was to get bread from the store. When I went in I was horrified to see the place crawling with rats. When I reported this back to the sergeant all he said was, "I never asked you for a health report. Go and get some bread."

There were rats everywhere, but the place where they congregated most was at the back of the camp. This was where the fire picket was located, and whilst there were firemen for the day shift we had to cover for night duty. On most night duties we were allowed to sleep, only being needed in case of an emergency. However, on fire picket duty it was impossible to sleep as there were rats everywhere. I remember trying to tuck my blanket round my feet as tightly as possible to prevent these vermin joining me in bed, only to find one under my pillow. Interestingly enough, the regular firemen were happy to be based there. As they saw it, no officer wanted to go near the place and so they were left largely to their own devices.

On 31st January and 1st February 1953 the east coast of Britain was devastated by flooding when hurricane winds combined with high tides. Clacton reported water levels of twelve feet and the overall death toll was 307. We were initially sent to Canvey Island in Essex, which was one of the worst hit areas where 58 people drowned. Later we went to Norfolk where there had been dozens of fatalities.

In Norfolk we were billeted in a wartime camp where the water was red with rust. Many of the lads were stricken with impetigo, an ugly skin disease brought on by the foul sanitary conditions and freezing weather. As if the disease was not obvious enough, you could see who had been affected by the tell-tale mauve stains of gentian violet, that great cure-all. The spread of impetigo became so severe that we were told we need not shave until further notice. Until this order came through we had been shaving with tea as it was the only hot liquid we had. In order to keep the billet warm at night we kept the boiler alight, but as this was fuelled by coke, I am sure that the gas it emitted did us far more harm than the cold ever would have.

It was our job to fill sandbags and we must have filled tens of thousands in the following weeks. This was more difficult than it sounds because what sand we could find was hidden under blankets of snow and was frozen solid. After eating lunch one day I washed my plate in the sea. It wasn't the blackness of the water which surprised me, but the fact that it froze the scraps of food solid on the plate.

The best place we could find to fill the sandbags was miles from anywhere. We felt totally isolated from the rest of humanity and the only people who bothered about us were the Salvation Army – we were immensely grateful when they arrived with cups of tea and other sustenance. Getting in the truck at night our uniforms steamed as the freezing air mixed with the perspiration from our exertions. It was an awful feeling, especially knowing that there was no luxury of a hot bath to follow.

As the water levels gradually reduced we were sent into towns to help clear sand from the houses. The water had been up to the roof in many instances and the ground floor rooms were carpeted in thick layers of sand.

Eventually we returned to Royston, by which time I had had enough. We had worked hard and had been of valuable assistance, but now the time was beginning to drag. I desperately wished that I had been among the fortunate ones, like Ron, who only had to do 18 months National Service, but sadly my intake was for two years. I took to counting down the months, weeks and days until it would all be over, and when that cherished day of demobilisation arrived it was not a second too soon.

The final weeks may have been a waste of time, but I valued the majority of my time in service, particularly with hindsight. I met people from all walks of life from all over the country. Never having left London, except for my brief evacuation to sleepy Hertfordshire, I found that living and working with all sorts of people, some of whom I would not have chosen to be with, was a great leveller.

When I was demobbed I saw the twins from Aldershot transit camp on the platform, the two who had been picked on by Corporal Bates. I was amazed at the transformation from the couple of wimps at the outset to the confident young sergeants standing before me. I hoped that National Service had done the same for me.

I was not yet totally free of my obligations, as National Servicemen were on emergency reserve for three years; we were even issued with a railway warrant to be used in the event of an emergency call-up. At the time I didn't give any of this much thought. I was out and could now get on with my own life... and after all, who would want Z Men who only had experience of sandbags and defunct tanks. However, three years later when the Suez Crisis reared its ugly head I was not quite so laid back. Ex-National Servicemen were being drafted on the basis of last out first back... I was relieved when the conscription stopped one short of my intake.

THINK OF A CARD...

Another condition of being on reserve meant having to attend a two-week refresher course each year. Attendance was compulsory, because if you did not turn up it was tantamount to desertion and you would be arrested. However, once there, the poor sergeants had little authority because we all knew we would be leaving in a matter of days. Backchat was rife, with some smart Alec at the far end of the inspection line giving it some verbal. When the sergeant went along to sort it out, another wise guy from the original end would join in. Upon arriving on one of the courses I was met with the words, "I bloody remember you, Lewin!" It was Sergeant Golding, and I remembered him, too, but at least it made for an entertaining fortnight!

When it came to going out on exercises we all did pretty well as we liked. I remember just lying in the long grass watching the poor sergeant trying to maintain some semblance of order, but it was a fiasco. The only consolation was meeting up with old mates, but as far as I was concerned it was a complete waste of time... and time was money.

Because I had never been posted further than one hundred miles from London it had been relatively easy for me to go back home whenever I had leave. I would catch up with the family and then usually have a few pints with some of my old mates. A few months after Mum had died I went to a dance in East Ham with some of these mates and it was there that I met Rose Palmer. Apart from her obvious good looks and great legs, I wonder if part of the attraction was that she had the same name as my mum.

Rose was a dress machinist from similar East End stock as myself. Her father, Jim, was an affable and generous docker who earned good money. He often slipped me five shillings before I went back to camp, which was appreciated because National Service pay was not good and I had no means of earning a few bob on the side. Of the 25 shillings I got each week from the government I tried to send one pound home, so it didn't leave much scope for socialising. Indeed, when I went home on a 48-hour pass I would usually arrange to meet Rose inside the cinema as I felt embarrassed that I was not able to pay for her ticket as well as my own. Rose understood my financial predicament and was quite happy to appease me in this manner.

We got on extremely well and Rose regularly sent me letters, which were particularly appreciated when I was working in the frozen wastes of Norfolk. I cannot admit to being quite such a good correspondent although I did try to put pen to paper at least once a week. I suppose I might have sent her a card from time to time... if there had been any decent card shops around! On reflection, I am glad there weren't any!

When I was demobbed in August 1953 I decided against going back to live with Dad. He had remarried about a year after Mum's death, which I felt was insensitive, although with hindsight I can appreciate his position. He and Mum had been so united in all they did that it must have been like losing his right arm. He couldn't function by himself and so I should not have been surprised that he would want to get settled again. He had depended on Mum so much for everything that the thought of being alone scared him. Even so, when he remarried I found it difficult to come to terms with, as did my brother and sister.

Dad was quite a catch as he was doing well for himself with his *Lucky Chimney Sweep* car hire business and he always took great pride in his appearance. He married Freda, a divorcee from Yorkshire. Freda had a sixteen-year-old daughter called Shirley, who sadly died the year after they married.

Tel and Ron offered me a room in their terraced house in Ilford. Alan was also living with them as Tel had taken him under her wing when Mum died. He was only nine at the time and so Tel naturally became his surrogate mother. Initially Alan and I shared a room, but this arrangement would not last for long as I had other plans. I wanted to ask Rose to marry me but I didn't have the money for an engagement ring. I had gone back to work at *Hicks & Son* until I could find something else to do, but I could see that it would be a long time before I had sufficient cash to buy Rose the sort of ring I felt she deserved. However, the solution was handed to me on a plate when Rose lent me her bike so that I could cycle to work. Jack Hicks was looking for a present for his daughter's birthday and asked if I was willing to sell the bike. I told him I was if the price was right. The £18 I got was enough to buy a ring, and by the time Rose noticed her bike was missing she didn't have the heart to say anything. Her dad was none too pleased, though, as he had bought her the bike!

Rose and I were married in December 1953 and even though the war had been finished for over eight years Britain was still experiencing considerable austerity – indeed, some rationing was still in force. We therefore had a quiet wedding, which suited us. It probably also suited Rose's parents because they paid for the wedding. The reception was held at a local school hall and Ron and

I sorted out the booze. As usual, there was not enough and so in true East End fashion we had a whip-round to see us through until we were chucked out. It was then back to my new in-laws' house where the party continued until 6 o'clock the following morning. Rose and I never did get to bed that night because after clearing up the mess from the party we caught a bus back to Ron and Tel's. We crashed out for most of Sunday and on Monday morning it was back to work... so much for a honeymoon.

Rose and I had a 'put-u-up' in the lounge at the front of the house. We made the room comfortable and furnished it as best we could, but it wasn't huge and so we were limited in what furniture we could have. However, Tel and Ron were very understanding and even allowed us to put an oven in the upstairs bathroom so that we could have a degree of privacy and not have to share their kitchen.

In the house opposite were a young couple who didn't seem to realise that, even though they had net curtains, everything could be seen as they always undressed with the light on. One evening we called Tel and Ron to come and watch the show. Rose and I were standing on the bed to get a better view and they climbed on too. We all thought it was very funny seeing this couple prancing around, but the laugh was on us when our put-u-up could no longer take our weight, folding in on itself and trapping us in the process. It must have looked quite an odd sight as we struggled to free ourselves... I only hope the couple over the road weren't watching! Poetic justice perhaps!

3 | Becoming a Salesman

By the time we got married I had moved out of the building trade. I had enjoyed the work, but I just knew that I would end up in selling. I had caught the bug as a boy and it was now part of my life. What's more, I wanted to be my own boss and I saw selling as a means of achieving that.

After National Service I thought it would be easy to get into selling, but here again I came across a reluctance to accept a chap without any qualifications. Enthusiasm is surely worth far more than bits of paper and I have always conducted my interviews for salesmen simply by having a chat. It's easy to tell who's got what it takes, and to my mind no amount of letters after your name are of any use in selling – if you don't have the gift of the gab and the personality then forget it.

A few weeks before Rose and I were married I got a job selling brushes door-to-door with *Kleeneze* and I only got this because it was commission only. However, the job suited me as it meant that if I didn't sell, we didn't eat... and it was my intention that we could afford to eat well. Selling door-to-door is the best groundwork for any budding salesman as it soon lets you know if you've got what it takes. When I had a good day I would feel as high as a kite, but I also had to learn how to take the bad days – and there were plenty of those.

I was given my patch and a huge case to hump around. This contained a whole assortment of brushes – everything from toothbrushes to brooms, as well as various cleaning materials like dusters and polish. The products were not cheap, but they were of high quality and that counted for something.

My initial aim would always be to sell the broom as, at about 35 shillings, this was the highest value item and provided me with the best commission. I just carried around the head of the broom which would then be attached to the handle with a wing nut. It had been designed to fit at different angles and so was more versatile – at least that was what I told my potential customers.

Once I had secured an order I sent the paperwork to the office and could then pick up the goods the following Friday. I would make my deliveries on the Friday night and during Saturday. *Kleeneze* had specifically arranged it this way as Friday was pay-day for the vast majority of people, and as this was always cash there was a far greater chance of being paid than if deliveries were made after the weekend.

When I delivered the brushes I used to try and make an extra sale, maybe something smaller like a tin of polish at 4s.6d. which I found was a good line, especially after pay-day when there were an extra few shillings in the purse. As I was on 20% commission, that was the best part of another shilling for me.

The thought of a salesman with a company car was unheard of in the 1950s and so it was a bus for me before trudging the streets of Upton Park, Forest Gate, Manor Park and Ilford. However, I soon realised that a car would help enormously with my deliveries and after a few months I had been able to save enough to buy a 1936 *Hillman Minx* for the princely sum of £100. The thought of using the car for going door-to-door never entered my head. The car was only ever used for deliveries and Monday morning saw me back in the queue at the bus stop.

Occasionally customers would change their minds and decide they did not want what they had ordered. This was always annoying, especially as I had effectively paid *Kleeneze* for the goods. I just had to accept that this was part of the job and set myself the target of selling the product to someone else as soon as possible. This was not particularly difficult as they had the advantage of taking immediate delivery.

I was starting to make good money and would be disappointed if I didn't clear £30 a week. *Kleeneze* had salesmen throughout the country, divided into regions. Incentives would be dangled in front of us for the best salesman in the region and it was not uncommon for me to pick up a tea set or perhaps a set of glasses at our monthly meetings. However, these were just a bonus; I made no bones about it – I was in it for the money.

That's not to say I didn't enjoy my work. Success breeds success and once you've got the bug there's always the desire to do better. However, I soon learned that there is such a thing as trying too hard. Having suffered several setbacks, perhaps having gone a street or two without having made a sale, it was important not to over-compensate by being pushy as this rarely worked. Also, many's the time I talked too much and actually talked myself out of the sale. I would try to learn from this, but I wasn't immune from making the same mistake again. Selling is all about confidence and I found that if I was starting to over-sell I might just as well get the bus back home and start again fresh the next day.

With hindsight I suppose it was easier to sell door-to-door in the 1950s than it would be today. For a start, very few women worked and so there was a good chance of someone being in. Also, people tended to be far more polite and trusting then and I am sure I made many a sale because the housewife felt sorry for me having to lug around a huge case and sell brushes for a living.

If offered a drink, I always accepted as it would give me more time to get to know the customer – it was always good to know people. I remember that for some reason I got talking to a lady about wine-making. This was one of her interests, so she offered me a glass of her home-brew. Naturally I accepted and was given a glass of potato wine, which was surprisingly good. I stood at the door talking for a while, but when I walked back down the garden path – thankfully having made a sale first – I felt very woozy and had to call it a day. As I made my way home on the bus I was annoyed with myself. I hated thinking I had lost a day's money, but at least I had learned a lesson and I never again accepted alcohol when selling door-to-door.

We never had any sales training, but I soon learned that, above all, whatever else I was selling, I was selling myself. I therefore always made sure that I was well presented, wearing a suit, clean collar and tie. I polished my shoes every day; having done my National Service, this came as second nature and was an invaluable discipline.

I was always polite and even decided that it was time to work on my speech. I was aware of my East End accent and tried to refine it.

Don't get me wrong – I was not ashamed of my roots and never will be. It's just that I was conscious that my use of English was not as good as it could be. If I could make more sales by being careful how I spoke, it would be worthwhile. I started by trying to eliminate 'ain't' from my vocabulary. I suppose that trying to better myself in this way could have been a throwback to Mum and Dad's influence.

I saw selling as a career, not just a job, and treated it in that professional manner. Right from the start I kept notes about every door I knocked on. If they were out I might arrange to go back at another time, but if they were out twice during the day it was likely that the wife was at work. This was a fair assumption as very few young people lived alone. Just about everyone got married straight from living with their parents and it was virtually unknown to come across a single mother – if for some reason the marriage had broken down each partner would go back to living with Mum and Dad... they couldn't afford not to.

If I spoke to the resident, even if nothing was bought, I would make notes. Sometimes I felt that they had given encouragement and might be worth visiting again, or else I would make notes to the effect that any further visit would be a waste of time. If I got to know their name this would also be recorded. When I made a sale there was even more to write down, especially if I had learned the names of the children or any other details which might be useful. I would read these notes before I visited the next time and this always gave me something to talk about and showed concern. It also meant that I was building a detailed picture of the area which might come in useful later... as I already had other ideas.

THINK OF A CARD...

There were times, however, when my professional mask dropped, one such occasion being when I delivered a deck scrubber to a grocer's shop. This was a good seller to shops as it had a sharp edge for cleaning the lino, the usual floor covering in such establishments. I was chatting amiably to the lady whilst looking for an opportunity for a follow-up sale. Her husband could not have been happy with the time she was giving me because he made some sarcastic remark to the effect that I had 'a nice mouthful of china', insinuating that I had false teeth. Now I am quite proud of my teeth. I agree that they did appear unusually white, but they were definitely all my own and I had no hesitation in telling him so. He repeated that they were not mine, upon which I told him he had a 'bloody cheek' and to put his money where his mouth was.

He put half a quid on the counter, and then followed what must have been quite a bizarre sight to anyone in the shop as I invited him to check if my teeth were false. Needless to say, he could not dislodge them. I thanked his wife for being so nice, thanked him for his donation to the Lewin fund and took my leave. I was pleased that I'd made ten bob, but also felt incensed about the whole charade. I never did understand what was behind it all. There again, perhaps it was worth ten bob just to get rid of me!

Selling door-to-door had many advantages, especially when the weather was fine. I enjoyed meeting people, I was effectively my own boss and when things were going well it was great. However, I was aware that I was only as good as my last week's pay, and after 18 months or so I felt it was time to look around for something where I could build more of a future.

For some time I had been thinking about selling credit – or 'the tally' as it was known. Having established a good round with *Kleeneze* I felt that it had the potential for such development as I was on good terms with dozens of customers already. I knew of a chap who had a credit business and approached him about my idea.

Mr Frank Ford already had an established reputation, having about ten agents working for him in the East London and Essex area. He usually developed new rounds from scratch with the help of canvassers, and so being offered a ready-made round he could see the merits of my proposition. It also helped that we hit it off well together and I think Frank admired my cheek in approaching him in this way. Whatever it was, he offered me a basic wage of £8 a week, plus commission on both sales and collections, and also said that I would be given a company van. He was just about to take a month's holiday and told me that I could start upon his return.

I was delighted because I hadn't expected a basic wage and so saw this as a generous offer. I accepted on the spot and told him I would hand in my notice at *Kleeneze* immediately. This I did but as I was told to just clear my current orders and then leave, I found myself with at least three weeks with nothing to do. I did not consider taking the time off between jobs – it was not the thing people did, and anyway I couldn't afford to as we needed the money, so I looked for something to occupy my time before I started my new venture.

I was lucky to get a job on a baker's round – they had a man off sick and I suited their requirements perfectly. I worked for Len Hirtes, one of three brothers who ran a chain of about 14 shops started by their father. One of these shops was on the 'Golden Mile' in Romford, so they were clearly doing well. My job was essentially that of a door-to-door bread salesman, with commission on anything extra I sold. I drove round in an electric van shouting, "Baker, Baker, Baker" to catch the attention of any potential customers – it was good fun. I soon saw that there was no margin in selling bread and rolls; the real money was to be made in pushing the biscuits and fancy cakes. Apparently the boss had to organise overtime to pay for the increased demand and was sorry to see me leave at the end of my three weeks. He even offered me quite a substantial rise to stay, but I had given my word to Frank Ford and was keen to work on the tally.

Credit selling was a very simple concept. It allowed people to buy what they wanted and then spread the payments over a number of months. A small amount of interest was charged for this facility, in much the same way as catalogues operate today. It was the job of the tallyman to make weekly collections and at the same time to sell and encourage a bit more business. It wasn't much of a tallyman who let a customer go, because once someone had got used to paying three or four bob a week, it was relatively easy to suggest they bought something else and just continue with the same payment. Of course, the aim was to increase the payment where possible, but not to the extent where the customer was overstretched.

Ford's principally offered clothes, soft furnishings and household goods, although in theory what we didn't have we could buy in for the customer. I remember taking some of my regulars to a local warehouse to buy three-piece suites or other furniture. The customer chose what she wanted and I wrote up her book. Frank had arrangements with many high quality outlets. He would make on the credit, and part of this was passed on to the salesman. We offered virtually everything... I even sold a wedding ring 'on tick'.

This was a very popular means of shopping because it must be remembered that few people had bank accounts, and even if they did loans were not usually available without some sort of security. Hire purchase was only in its infancy, involving stringent credit checks which excluded most people, and also there was no such thing as a credit card. In the mid-1950s the country was still emerging from wartime austerity... indeed, rationing only finished in 1954. The tally offered people the chance to buy what were usually necessities, plus a few luxuries, and spread payment into affordable instalments.

I always kept a reasonable amount of basic stock in my van, but would often be asked to bring along, for example, a pair of black size 9 shoes, when I came the following week. I would take along a choice of three pairs, maybe lace-ups, brogues and a pair of slip-ons, and usually they would choose at least one pair, sometimes two. This might not seem like a wide choice today but even the shops would not have carried a much more extensive selection.

Frank soon realised that I had a flair for selling and gave me end of lines to get rid of; the incentive was a larger commission. It might be dresses, towels, sheets, doormats; whatever it was I was up for the challenge and usually sold it in pretty quick time.

Getting into selling credit was a good move for me as it offered repeat business which is always easier than cold calling. I also made many friends and was often regarded as one of the family. More than once I was shown a child's school book which had reference to "...Uncle Don coming to visit us on Friday night." Sometimes a lady might run three or four books for her mum and sisters. I also had plenty of customers where I supplied the children once they'd married and left home.

As with the selling of brushes, Friday nights and Saturdays were busy times for us to coincide with pay-day. To compensate for this we had Thursdays off, but even then I used to work, sometimes going round with the canvassers to learn more about selling. Now these men were something different – they really knew how to sell and used every trick in the book. There was one man in particular called Joe – if he couldn't make a sale, no one could. If he was selling saucepans, as soon as the door was open he'd start flinging saucepan lids into the hall saying something like, "There they are Girl. All for you and only two bob a week." Few women would be able to say 'No' as he was so cheeky. Also, they were unable to close the door on him as they had his lids in their hall. Alternatively, he might be holding a picture or mirror and as soon as the door was opened he would walk straight past the lady and start positioning the frame on the wall, saying, "That's where it should be Girl. I've brought it just for you and it's only two bob a week."

It would be Joe's job to get a customer on the book and take the first payment. Thereafter the customer was passed to the tallyman to look after. Of course, these tactics were sometimes counter-productive as they might end in bad debts. This would make my job much more difficult and, apart from leaving a sharpened matchstick wedged in the doorbell when I knew there was someone at home who was not answering the door, there was little else I could do. The debts just had to be written off. Sometimes I would go to a house where the letters 'D S' were scrawled on the door. They stood for

'Don't Serve' and usually meant that I was wasting my time even trying to get an answer.

I preferred to get my customers by personal recommendation and usually this was the case. However, my greatest problem was getting through my round on a Friday night because I was often invited in for a cuppa and a chat; it was not uncommon for it to be midnight before I got home on such evenings. Strangely, even though I might be carrying £300-£400 on a Friday night, I never came across any trouble. Much of my work was on council estates and in some of the less well-heeled areas, but I never felt uncomfortable. This was my world and I was among friends.

Ford's was a good company to work for and I was treated well. In fact, I was considered one of the family and I certainly saw Frank as a father figure. I looked up to him and admired his integrity and his manner. He was well spoken, which impressed me and made me resolve to try harder to remove more of my East End coarseness. Whilst Mr Ford was a physically big man he had a presence about him that had nothing to do with his stature. He had been born in Forest Gate and had made good; perhaps I saw some of my own father in him, although I probably still wasn't ready to admit it at this stage.

I hadn't been working long for Mr Ford when Rose and I decided we had to do something about our accommodation. Living with Tel and Ron was enjoyable, but it was unsatisfactory, especially as Alan was getting to the stage where he also needed his own space. I was still only 21 but I wanted a place of my own. I wasn't sure how I was going to do it, but I was ambitious and that was half the battle. Rose was also a hard worker, and despite working in the traditionally low paid rag trade, because she was on piecework she brought home a very useful wage. I was earning good money and I knew that between us we could easily afford a mortgage; we just had to convince the Council of that, and come by a deposit from somewhere. We had grown accustomed to having money and to saving it, but we had not saved as much as we would have liked.

None of this would actually have been much of a problem if we had set our sights on something small in one of the less desirable areas of town, but that wasn't my style, or at least not the style to which I wanted to become accustomed. I was setting my sights on something better than I could really afford and I convinced myself that it was the right thing to do. We looked around and found an ideal house in St Leonard's Gardens, Ilford, at what seemed to be a remarkably reasonable price, £2,000. It had been built in 1938 and was a large three-bedroom end terrace with a garage and garden. It was in a good location and as far as I was concerned it was ideal, especially as it was in need of a bit of attention, which was reflected in the price and also meant that we might be able to make a bit of money on it.

Even though I had been working with Frank for only a few months I had an inkling that he would be prepared to help out with a deposit. My faith was well founded and so Rose and I arranged to have a look round what we hoped might become our own house.

We were shown round by the tenant – I got the feeling that she did not want to move but was rather resigned to the fact that she would have to. I can't say that she was rude, but she certainly didn't go out of her way to make us feel welcome. My first impression was one of total amazement; how could such a new house be allowed to get into such a state of disrepair? There was a hole right back to the brick by the front door and the state of the decor was shabby to say the least.

We only found out later, although by now we had our suspicions, that this 'lady' was of a rather dubious profession. It appeared that she and her various 'clients' had their minds on more interesting matters than worrying about the upkeep of fixtures and fittings!

With my background in jobbing building I could see the potential of the place and so despite its colourful past we made an offer, which was accepted. We joked to ourselves that at least the neighbours would welcome us with open arms once they satisfied themselves that we wouldn't be having all-night parties. Thankfully, we never had any unannounced nocturnal visitors, nor did we find a stash of red light bulbs.

Frank agreed to lend us £100, Rose's dad £50 and with our own savings we had the 10% deposit required. Even though I only had a relatively small basic wage, I was able to convince the Council that a 90% mortgage was well within our means and the mortgage offer was duly made, 4% over 25 years. However, there were certain conditions: the chimney stack had to be re-pointed and the back of the house re-pebble dashed. We were allowed to move in and were given six months in which to carry out the work.

Moving in didn't take much effort; after all we only had a roomful of furniture. However, we were soon able to start getting things together thanks to Aunt Lou, who gave us a double bed, and Mrs Eyre, my friend's mother, who gave us a wardrobe. A customer in Dagenham had just bought a new carpet to replace one which was threadbare in the middle, and she said I could have the old one if I wanted. This was ideal for us as we put it in the bedroom; the bed covered the worn patch and as the edges of the carpet were unmarked it was like new. I also managed to scrounge an old broken down TV, which, once covered with a cloth, made a useful bedside table.

Although we had plenty of space we didn't need any furniture for upstairs as we had agreed to let that to a friend of Rose's. Betty and Steve were saving up for a place of their own and were happy to rent our three upstairs rooms as well as sharing our bathroom. There was one other condition – that they decorate upstairs. I knew that Steve's dad was a decorator and, just as I had hoped, he was happy to lend a hand!

As I had a company van I decided I didn't need the garage, so I let this to a friend of Tel's – he was a paint salesman needing somewhere to store his stock. He paid me ten bob a week, and as our mortgage was only £9.5s. a month, with Betty and Steve's 30 shillings a week it meant that we only had to find 25 shillings a month. I was well pleased and didn't even mind having to tackle the chimney and pebble dashing. With my brief experience of the building trade I was soon able to knock that off over a couple of weekends. In fact, I quite got into DIY and painted the outside of the house while I was at it.

Even though this was a lovely house, we didn't intend to stay long. It was already clear to me that property was a good investment and I simply saw this as a stepping stone to something better. As it transpired, we were to have ten addresses over the next 20 years, each time working on the property to add to its value and taking a small step up the ladder... however, now I'm getting ahead of myself.

Whilst living in St Leonard's Gardens I got to know our local grocer, a decent chap by the name of Ted Powell. He had a shop on Ilford Lane and we just hit it off – for that matter, so did Rose and his wife Kathy. Whenever I popped in Ted and I would invariably end up discussing business ideas and generally putting the world to rights. One day he said that he and Kathy would like to take us out to dinner and a date was arranged. The interesting thing was that despite being in our twenties, married and buying our own house, neither Rose nor I had ever been to a restaurant before.

Ted drove in his lovely *Morris Oxford*, taking us to the *Lyons Corner House* in Charing Cross Road. There were dozens of *Lyons Corner Houses* all over the country, but I believe the one in Charing Cross Road was a bit special. It even boasted a Palm Court orchestra with all the musicians wearing dinner suits – they were better dressed than me! I was bowled over by the place, the opulence and splendour being something I'd only ever seen before in the films.

We sat down at our table and were waited on by an elegant 'Nippy' in her smart black dress with white lace apron and bonnet, but what stunned me most was the amount of cutlery on the table – I only had two hands for goodness sake! I felt embarrassed, but Ted was great. He realised that Rose and I were not accustomed to such surroundings and he gently took us under his wing, explaining what all the cutlery was for and how to tackle it... from the outside working in! I can't remember what I had to eat – probably the same as Ted, and I also let Ted deal with the wine, as I wouldn't have had a clue what to order, although I certainly approved of his choice. Ted was not a snob, he just liked the finer things in life and he enjoyed spoiling us. We certainly enjoyed it too, and if all went well, perhaps Rose and I would be able to eat out more often in the future... perhaps even being able to afford to treat Ted and Kathy.

We had always had dogs when I was growing up, so when Rose and I were nicely settled into our new house we discussed the idea of getting one. I love Alsatians as they have a great temperament and so I went to see about one in Bedford. As all dog owners will testify, you know the dog for you as soon as you set eyes on it, and this was certainly the case with Ricky. He was soon one of the family, and I really enjoyed taking him for a walk at whatever time I got home in the evening; it was one of the few times I could really relax.

During the day Ricky stayed in the kitchen, although we left the back door open so he could go into the garden whenever he wanted. People didn't worry about leaving their back door unlocked, and with Ricky about the chances of any burglar wanting to break in were pretty remote. Even if they did, we had nothing worth taking – in fact, I used to say they would probably leave us a few bob!

We soon discovered just how good a guard dog Ricky was when the pub next-door had their fence fixed. The workmen needed to come into our garden to do some of the work, which would have been fine in the normal course of events. It's just that they hadn't reckoned on Ricky. I knew nothing of all this until I came home at about 5 o'clock that evening. Rose was not yet back home and I was surprised not to have Ricky bounding up at me when I went into the kitchen. It was then that I heard shouting coming from the garden shed. Upon investigating, I discovered two workmen. They had been there all day, Ricky making sure they didn't escape – they made it clear they weren't going to take any chances, however long they had to sit there! They were not very happy, but Ricky had only been doing his job.

During these years I never took much holiday, not that there was much to take as most people only got two weeks' paid annual leave… the good old days from an employer's point of view! Many times I did not even take both weeks, usually having one week off and taking pay for the second. However, by the late 1950s things were looking up and so we decided to go abroad, a pretty sophisticated thing to do at the time even if our destination was only Jersey. Rose looked and dressed like Doris Day, which made me feel like I had a film star on my arm as we boarded the plane for our first ever flight. I remember that well. It was a big, four engine propeller plane that made my ears sing and I was deaf for hours after landing.

Having so enjoyed our 'foreign holiday' to Jersey, the following year Rose and I decided to be even more adventurous, choosing a package holiday to San Remo in Italy with Ron and Tel. We had a great time, and I also remember buying a few watches on the cheap from one of the street traders. I was able to sell these back in England and help pay for the holiday!

Before going on the Jersey holiday I booked Ricky into the local kennels; we were living in Epping by then. Ricky was 13 by this time and had been having some health problems, but in between he was as lively as a three-year-old. When we returned from Jersey I went to pick up Ricky, only to be met with the devastating news that he had been put to sleep because he had been so ill. It took me a long time to get over the death of this special friend.

Our next dog, again an Alsatian, was Sheena, the most intelligent dog I've ever come across – I swear she knew everything you said.

I'm moving forward a few years here, but I particularly remember the games of hide and seek she played with our daughter, Debbie, who was about seven at the time. Debbie and her friends would hide then one of them would shout out, "Ready." Sheena would wander round and find them all – it didn't matter whether there were three children or ten, Sheena would know how many and always find them. She could be quite aggressive towards strangers, and even bit someone once, but thankfully Sheena was always fantastic with the children, never giving us any cause to worry.

Other Alsatians over the years have been Bonnie, Benjie and, more recently, Bessie. Barney is my current best friend, but he is not the only Alsatian around because the police use a couple of my fields for training their dogs. I love watching these beautiful animals being put through their paces, so majestic and powerful, yet so obedient. I have the greatest respect for them and their handlers.

During my years with *Ford's* I was getting along quite nicely. I had dozens of lovely customers, many of whom I would call friends. I saw their children growing up and people pass on and I felt I belonged. I also enjoyed the money. I was earning a reasonable income, certainly enough to move every couple of years or so and even to buy a car. I remember the thrill of sitting in my own brand new *Vauxhall Wyvern* and feeling as if I owned the road. However, despite all this, I still wasn't satisfied. I was working for someone else when really I wanted to be working for myself.

Frank Ford had hinted several times at the possibility of me buying my own round, but whenever I raised the subject I could sense that he was hedging. I had been working for Frank for six years now and I decided it was time to take matters into my own hands and force a decision one way or the other.

Early in the New Year of 1961 Rose informed me she was pregnant with our first child. We had agreed that the time was right to start a family and I was delighted with the news. However, at the same time it made me realise that life was moving on and I wasn't. It was the kick up the backside I needed and I knew it had to be now or never if I was to strike out in business on my own.

I had been keeping my eye on a gents' outfitters in Woodford Green for some time. I knew that it was coming up for sale and saw it as the perfect place for redevelopment. It would tie in nicely with the tally business as I could sell some of the stock on the rounds, and hopefully encourage customers to come in to pay their weekly dues, thereby saving time. I had big plans for my own tally business and this was just the first step. I worked out my sums, but it all depended on how much Frank charged me for my round. I would have to act quickly to secure the shop, so again I asked Frank for a price. When he stalled I realised that he was never going to sell me the round. If I wanted to continue in the tally business, I would have to start from scratch on my own and so I had to let the shop go. Frank and I parted on good terms – we had both done well out of the relationship, but now it was time for me to move on.

I knew I had the confidence to be my own boss – after all, when working on commission only it amounts to the same thing. I also knew that I could sell. I just wanted to be pointed in the right direction to start marching off under my own steam... but in what direction?

THINK OF A CARD...

As if such decisions were not significant enough, other life-changing events were happening at this time, because in August 1961 our son was born, giving me even greater incentive to be the provider. Incidentally, I should explain how his name came about as the question has cropped up many times over the years. Our son was named Clinton after Clint Walker, a giant of a man and the eponymous hero Cheyenne Bodie in the cult TV western, *Cheyenne*, which ran for over a hundred episodes from the mid-1950s until 1963. I loved the programme, but cannot remember seeing too many episodes in the latter years because there was always so much work to do. It was considered pretty sophisticated to have a television set then, and video recorders were still a long way in the future!

A few days after Rose had given birth I was visiting her in hospital when she happened to mention that she didn't have a wristwatch. She was not dropping a hint, like she might when we had a bit more money to spare – it was just a comment in passing. Things were very tight at the time but I wanted to spoil her. After all, she had just given birth to our first child, in addition to which she always supported my hare-brained ideas and put up with me being a workaholic, out of the house for umpteen hours a day.

I calculated what I could afford, and after allowing for what I owed, I had the princely sum of eight quid. I could get a lovely watch for a fiver and still have a bit of spare cash for emergencies. I looked in the windows of a couple of jewellers, but nothing really appealed except for a beautiful watch priced at... you've guessed it, eight pounds. I knew I had no option and so I bought the watch. It left me absolutely boracic, but I felt like the king of England when

I gave Rose the presentation box, beautifully wrapped by the jeweller. It's strange, but since then I have been able to spoil Rose and spend considerably more money on her, but nothing gave me greater pleasure than buying her that watch. It had cost me everything I had, and you can't give more than that, but Rose was worth it and she still is.

Happy Birthday Don

'One day, Rose, we'll
all be millionaires'

4 | On the Cards

I started to look in various trade papers, but it's difficult looking when you're not sure what it is you are looking for. One advertisement in the *Daily Telegraph* read, "Agent wanted to sell remainder greeting cards." I knew nothing about greeting cards, but I was interested in the prospect of being an agent. It would mean that I could run my own patch and be my own boss. It also meant that I would be able to work from home.

I replied to the ad and was invited to the *Whitehouse Hotel* in London to meet Abba Rivlin and Maurice Fern. They had travelled down from Leeds where they ran a company called *Mayflower Gambitt* which sold greeting cards to wholesalers. They had obviously done quite well for themselves if appearances were anything to go by and they certainly came across as being honourable gentlemen, something borne out time and time again over the following years. They had spotted a niche in the market for remainder cards – those they had not been able to sell to the wholesalers. The cards were brand new and well packaged, just surplus to requirements.

Abba and Maurice had already set up six outlets in the north of England for agents to sell cards directly to retailers. They would supply the agent with stock on sale or return. The agent in turn would sell the cards for cash and receive a 30% commission. They were looking to develop the business in the south of England with each agent developing whatever area he wanted. There was no ceiling on ability and the agent could employ sub-agents if he so wished.

The conversation was going well and so they produced a big concertina-like file containing dozens of different cards. They told me that this was a 'blad' and was the way to display a range of cards to a retailer. I could see that the cards were of a reasonable quality, but there was no reason why I should think otherwise, after all, a card was a card as far as I was aware. It was an accurate assumption because the concept of selling cards by quality was not a factor the market had yet embraced.

The range of cards was extensive and I could see little problem in being able to shift them. My confident attitude must have appealed to Abba and Maurice because they offered to take me on as their agent. I don't know if any of the other applicants were successful that day, but I was promised the London area and that was plenty big enough for me... well, for the time being at least!

I accepted immediately and they told me they would send down a small British Rail container, full of cards, to arrive the following Monday morning – that sounded like an awful lot of cards to me. In the meantime they gave me the blad and a price sheet and wished me luck. Now all I had to do was learn about the greeting card industry and familiarise myself with my merchandise... and I had a whole weekend in which to do so!

Like most people, I thought I knew a fair amount about cards – after all, what was there to know? If someone wanted a card they popped into a newsagents and hunted around until they found something vaguely appropriate – surely there was no great mystique about it.

The first thing I did was walk down the high streets of Romford and Ilford looking for any outlet which sold cards. Mostly they were newsagents or sweet shops, but I also came across a couple of smaller half-size shops, one of which sold wool and cards and another which sold handbags and cards.

It appeared that cards were a useful sideline, but it seemed they did not provide much of a return as they were given so little space. In one shop cards were given their own corner, but mostly they were to be found out of the way on a wire rack, or perhaps on some wooden shelving a couple of feet wide, but certainly not a display as we know them today. At best, cards would be in batches of the same theme, but in other outlets they were simply thrown into a box at random and it was up to the customer to search through until a suitable card was found.

Things were relatively simple at the time and there was not too much thought behind the marketing of cards; indeed marketing was a concept which did not really exist – certainly not in the greeting card business. Little did I appreciate how things were to change over the coming years, and that I was to be one of the principal architects behind that change.

My walk round the shops was not encouraging, but it all depended on the volume of cards sold and that was something I could not gauge until I started to do my rounds. I could see from my price list that there was a reasonable margin in selling cards, but without being able to match it against volume I was just clutching at straws. I decided that the rest of my time would be better spent learning about my products.

The blad was divided into sections for the different cards. The more popular cards were sold in batches, for example birthday and anniversary cards where a selection would be provided, whilst the more obscure categories would be sold in a miscellaneous bundle. The retailer would buy a box of cards which contained themes such as 'Congratulations on Passing your Exams', 'Get Well', 'Welcome to your New Home', 'With Deepest Sympathy' etc. Each of these would arrive in boxes containing between six dozen and four gross of cards.

The cards were printed by several different suppliers and I had to learn each range and the appropriate prices. I soon decided which ones I would prefer to sell because of the margin, but I had yet to see what would be the most popular with the retailers.

Rose was a tremendous help, and after I had done some homework and tried to educate myself with the greeting card industry, she sat for hours while I went through the merits of each selection, explaining why she should buy them... if only she'd had some money I am sure I could have retired that weekend.

Sure enough, on Monday morning a British Rail lorry drew up with a special delivery for me: a container with at least 200 boxes of cards. The first thing we had to do was find somewhere to store them, and that done I had to make up a dozen or so selection boxes to take with me – there were boxes of cards everywhere. I loaded up the car and off I went, a little apprehensive, but very excited.

I started off the way I meant to go on. I waited for a customer to leave the shop, after which I introduced myself to the manager and said, "I can sell you greeting cards cheaper than you can get anywhere in the country." This was quite a bold claim, but I knew it to be true. I was getting the cards for less than the wholesalers paid, but without the overheads, so it was easy to stand by my statement. Even by sticking to my price list most retailers could get the cards off me for less than they were currently paying. Additionally, most newsagents were popping along to the local cash and carry to buy a selection box of cards, and here was me making life easy for them by delivering to their premises.

I made a sale at that very first shop, and whilst it might only have been for £10-£15's worth of cards it gave me a tremendous boost and took away any lingering doubts I had about the direction of my new career. By the end of the day you would have thought I knew all about the industry I had just become part of – as far as my prospective clients were concerned, no one knew more about greeting cards than yours truly. I feel pretty confident in making that bold claim today, but back in 1963 this was perhaps a little premature.

Not every establishment accepted my sales pitch, even though I felt they were daft not to do so. Some shops already had a plentiful supply, others showed loyalty to their current supplier and a third group thought there must be a catch and could not bring themselves to trust me. They were following the old adage, 'If it seems too good to be true, it probably is.' However, I am pleased to say that in the weeks and months that followed most of these reservations were overcome by all but the most recalcitrant managers.

As I got to know my customers I started suggesting ways for them to increase their sales. This usually related to better presentation, which gave me considerable scope, especially as I had come across a supplier who could provide wire carousels. Initially I would provide one of these on a trial basis, knowing full well that increased sales would invariably result in me selling them the carousel on the next visit.

Occasionally reservations were about price. One manager complained that he had not sold any of the cards he had bought off me. I noticed that he was selling them at a much lower price than usual, 5d each, and so I advised that he put them up to a shilling. He was flabbergasted by this suggestion, but after a little persuasion took my advice. The next time I visited he placed a double order – he had sold out! I explained to him that it was all to do with perception of quality. If a card looks too good for the price at which it is being offered the customer will suspect something and more often than not steer clear. They are much more likely to buy if they feel they are buying quality. Coupled with that is the fact that in Britain people feel far more comfortable about spoiling others. If the more expensive cards were for themselves, more than likely they would not be able to justify the cost, but someone else was worth the extra.

At the time the greeting card business was unsophisticated, but now things are substantially different because of competition in the industry. This has benefited everyone because increasing the choice and quality of cards has also greatly expanded the number of cards sold. To my mind quality is now the most important factor, but this must still always be coupled with value for money.

I was also amazed at the lack of common sense shown by some shop owners. In the New Year newsagents were telling me that they had done well as they had sold out of Christmas cards two weeks before Christmas. I couldn't believe it! These were the chaps I was having a hard time trying to sell six dozen Valentine cards or three dozen Easter cards to. A pack of three dozen was only 36 cards for goodness sake. If they couldn't sell 36 cards over Easter in a Christian country they shouldn't be in business in the first place!

I could see that there was enormous scope for increased sales, especially as new ranges of cards were beginning to appear. What distressed me most was the dismissive attitude towards cards by many of the shop owners. It seemed that because the unit price was small they allocated little space to the displays – and using the word 'displays' is being kind. It was my contention that whilst the value of each sale may be small, if the mark-up was good and there were enough sales, profits would be significant. Furthermore, an attractive display of cards might encourage a customer to enter the shop in the first place – once in they then might buy something else, perhaps a magazine, so sales were further increased.

I had some minor successes with these conversations, but it struck me that if I felt so passionate about these ideas I would be better off pursuing them myself. However, all this had to be in the future. For the time being I had to sell cards and more cards to be able to finance my other plans.

My first few weeks were encouraging and I was learning all the time. Once they had gained more confidence, retailers were beginning to place orders for several boxes of cards at a time. Despite being rebuffed early on by some newsagents, I would pop back from time to time to see if they had softened at all – if I'm honest, I saw it as a challenge to get them on my books, and the harder they made it for me initially, the greater the challenge. I always remember one tough nut who barely gave me the time of day. I knew I'd cracked it when I went into his shop one day and he started the conversation with, "Hello old boy." A special moment! Interestingly, word was also beginning to spread and I started being approached by other newsagents looking to get in on the act.

The cards were sent from Leeds by train, and space was allocated by container. Initially I was given half a container, but later this increased to a whole container. The next step was to increase the frequency of orders, but this could only come with more salesmen.

I found one or two other chaps to help sell the cards. I gave them 20% commission, leaving 10% for myself, but even then it was touch and go as to whether the hassle was worth my while because I knew that in the time it took to attend to them, I could have earned more by selling the cards myself. It was only when I had four or five salesmen that I started to appreciate the benefit.

A typical day would involve being up early to collect a consignment of cards before going on my rounds selling to regular customers. Once the shops had shut I would then drive round to see a couple of the chaps I had working for me. Thankfully, traffic wasn't as bad at it is today, but it still took time to get to different parts of London. I would work out what they had sold, replenish their stock and review the finances. Once back home it was a case of sorting out the boxes of cards from that morning's delivery, putting them into manageable quantities for my own customers and for my co-workers. After that there was paperwork to be done, paying invoices to *Mayflower Gambitt* and deciding what new stock needed to be ordered. They were pretty long days, but hard work never killed anyone.

It must also be remembered that there were no such things as computers with email, text messages, mobile phones or even fax machines. Many of the chaps I had working for me didn't even have a phone at home, so they would leave messages with Rose if I was out. Contacting them was difficult and meant more meetings than would now be the case, but we knew no different and just got on with it.

Once in a blue moon I would pop up to Leeds to see Abba and Maurice and visit their massive warehouse, a converted cotton mill, to look at new stock. If they had a line which was not selling they might offer me better terms, but this did not mean that I would accept. I was becoming discerning about what cards would sell, and it was better to have a smaller margin with cards that sold rather than hold obsolete stock.

As I mentioned earlier, the main business of *Mayflower Gambitt* was selling cards to wholesalers, with reps all over the country. The cards I was given were end of lines, overruns and obsolete stock, so even though I was beginning to make some in-roads into the East London area, it was not going to impact their business. As they saw it, I was just increasing the market by selling to a few hundred newsagents. This having been said, Abba and Maurice could see that I had potential and they were keen to offer me some of their better lines. I remember seeing some beautiful boxed cards with an acetate cover. I thought these would be easy to sell, but it transpired that the acetate curled in the hot weather and I ended up having to give refunds – another lesson learned.

THINK OF A CARD...

Our meetings were always edifying and congenial, not least because they were pleased with the business I was generating. They were both very bright men and it came as no surprise to me when I learned that Abba was a Yorkshire chess champion – he certainly made some very shrewd moves. They would always invite me to have lunch with them, but I only agreed occasionally, after all, time was money – when I wasn't working I wasn't earning!

On the rare occasion when I did take an evening off to socialise, poor Rose had to put up with me talking shop all night. Everyone soon knew not to ask Don what he did for a living, because he would tell you... and two hours later he would still be telling you!

I lived and breathed work – I loved it. More importantly, I've always felt that you have to be this committed if you want to get anywhere in business. This also means taking opportunities as they arise, and making those opportunities in the first place. I remember talking to a chap called Roger at a party. We got on well and he was my sort of bloke – straight talking and a character. If you are to make a success of selling you have to have some sort of personality, and Roger had it by the bucketful. I soon sounded him out to see if he would like to work for me selling cards, and he turned out to be a natural. Eventually he ended up running one of my shops.

Whilst I was convinced that greeting cards could become a good business, I cannot claim to have had any great vision about the future at this early stage. If you had told me then that I would build a company of over 1,000 shops, employing 10,000 people with an annual turnover in excess of £500 million I would have said you were crackers. All I was interested in at this time was being able to support my family and my ambition to be rich! I had also set my sights on owning a *Rolls Royce,* but that would have to wait for now. Apart from these few modest aims I enjoyed the thrill of seeing a business grow, and I seemed to be reasonably good at that.

Part of growing a business is taking risks, or 'opportunities' as the spin-doctors call them today. When it is your own money, believe me it is a risk, but hopefully a calculated and informed risk. Another of these risks was rearing its head. It could not have escaped the notice of anyone in 1960s London that laundrettes were springing up all over place.

I am reliably informed that the first electric washing machine was invented by John W Chamberlain of the *Bendix Aviation Corporation* in the early 1930s. This machine could wash, rinse and drain water in a single operation – a potential godsend to housewives the world over, although the cost of such machines would make them prohibitive for domestic use for several decades to come. JF Cantrell was the enterprising chap who opened the first 'Washeteria' in Fort Worth, Texas in 1934 but it took some time for these to catch on. It was fifteen years before the idea crossed the Atlantic, the first 'Laundrette' being opened in London's Bayswater in 1949. Assistants charged 2s.6d. (12½p) per wash, with an extra penny for drying. 'Bag washes' were soon to be found all over London and other major cities, where laundry could be deposited and collected later that day all washed. It would probably still be damp, as drying cost extra. In 1960 the first fully automatic self-service laundrette was opened, launching a decade of liberation.

This coincided with Britain emerging from the drab and austere 1950s as the nation struggled to repay the national debt incurred by an economically ruinous war. The Festival of Britain on London's

South Bank had engendered a degree of optimism, and later in the decade Prime Minister Harold Macmillan was able to declare that, "… most of our people have never had it so good."

A further factor contributing to the success of the laundrette phenomenon was the population explosion. Added to the post-war 'baby-boom' was an influx of migrants to many cities, London in particular. As independence was granted in many former outposts of the British Empire, and with a huge demand for workers domestically, migrants arrived from all over the globe in their tens of thousands. There was work aplenty in the National Health Service, London Transport and to meet the demands of hungry road-building programmes. Additionally, builders were required to convert countless Victorian townhouses into flats and bedsits to accommodate these migrants.

Having been required to work during the war, many women were used to receiving a wage and liked the independence that came with it. New legions of working mums sought the freedom that labour-saving devices provided, and top of the list was the washing machine. Laundrettes couldn't open quickly enough, and most were full from dawn to dusk. I thought this must surely be a licence to print money and so had a word with my brother-in-law, Ron Saunders.

Ron had his own grocery shop, but he was up for the challenge and so we set about looking for potential sites. This was a whole new ballgame as far as I was concerned. Obviously we were keen to get the right shop, but we didn't want to appear so keen that we got ripped off. Also, what was the right area? Only time would tell.

We settled on a corner shop in Ilford, negotiated the rent and set about fitting it out. By this time we had visited countless laundrettes and decided on *Westinghouse* top-loaders which could hold up to 14lb of clothes. We also bought six dryers and two dry-cleaning machines. We were all set and confidently predicted making our fortunes... but it didn't work out quite like that.

We opened on a Saturday, but I went to work that morning selling cards as usual. I had had a good morning, so clocked off early from the cards to pop along and see how our new goldmine was faring. I stopped off at home first to collect Rose so that she, too, could share in the excitement. When we got to the laundrette it was late afternoon but we had only taken £4.10s. all day. Our outlay had been considerable and we were tied into various agreements so this was looking serious – where had we gone wrong? It had seemed like a promising location, but looking out in the street there were surprisingly few people around... it was like a ghost town. It was then that the penny dropped – this was a predominantly Jewish area and here we were opening our shop on the Sabbath. No wonder business was slow. The next day, a Sunday, the laundrette was packed, as it was every other day, and we had a thriving business.

I have never been opposed to working long hours, but having a laundrette took things to a new dimension. To maximise revenue, the laundrette had to be open seven days a week, from first thing in the morning until late at night – the later the better. Many customers liked to take advantage of the late hours, and at such times there was often a community feel to the place as regulars got to know each other. We employed a couple of assistants to look after things during the day, and also to wash, dry and fold the clothes for busy working mums. A modest fee was charged for this service, but due to its popularity the cost of the assistants was more than covered.

After closing time the laundrette had to be cleaned, and I was also surprised by the amount of maintenance required, both to the machines and to the boiler room. At this rate we were going to have to invite the engineer to the Christmas party! I remember waiting for the engineer to call one Sunday. There were a few people in the laundrette and Ron was in the boiler room tinkering about with something or other. I was passing the time of day with a customer when, all of a sudden, there was a loud explosion out back and the sight of Ron being propelled past me. He had been blown clean out of the boiler room, emerging looking somewhat dazed and with his eyebrows singed. Poor Ron, whatever his condition, all we could do was laugh. Fortunately, he was OK and it was not long before he could see the funny side of it too.

On another occasion I remember we had problems with one of the dry-cleaning machines – we couldn't stop the blasted thing. Now the purpose of the dry-cleaner was to treat delicate fabrics and so the clothes tended to be a cut above those bundled into the all-purpose washing machines. This poor lady had inserted her precious garments hours before, yet here was the machine still running. From our point of view, whilst it was stuck it wasn't earning money, so neither of us was happy with the situation. I told the lady that I would get the machine fixed and suggested that she come back in an hour. This she did, but I was no further forward and the engineer hadn't arrived, so I suggested another hour... followed by another hour... and another. I was getting more embarrassed every time she appeared. It was 2 o'clock in the morning before her clothes were finally extricated, remarkably none the worse for wear... and they were certainly very clean. I suppose it would have been a bit churlish of me to have charged her for the whole time she had been using the machine!

Another late night I recall was when I was trying to get some curtains dry for a customer. They were of a heavy dralon material and the dryer seemed to be making precious little headway. What's more, they smelled badly of the percoethylene dry-cleaning fluid, the fumes of which could floor you! Fortunately it was a warm summer evening so I took the curtains out into the backyard and hung them over the line to dry... so much for technology!

As business progressed, and having learned the ropes, Ron and I decided to open another laundrette in Romford, which Ron kept an eye on. Of course, all the while we were running our other operations, Ron his grocer's, and me full-time on the cards and looking after the sub-agents. However, after a couple of years of this Ron realised that diversifying was too demanding for him and so we decided to sell the laundrettes. Despite making a good return on our investment, I still learnt a valuable lesson – stick to what you know best, and for me this was greeting cards.

I decided the time had come to put my theories to the test about opening a dedicated greeting card shop. I had worked for myself for five or six years by now and felt I knew everything there was to know about selling cards. Had I realised then how little I knew compared with what I have picked up over the last 40 years perhaps I would have had second thoughts, but the innocence of ignorance and the enthusiasm of youth are wonderful.

THINK OF A CARD...

I wasn't daft enough to burn all my boats, especially as I had eight men working for me selling cards to newsagents, so I had a word with Abba and Maurice, who were as understanding as I expected them to be – after all, they had nothing to lose.

I don't think Rose was best-pleased when I announced my latest idea, not that she said anything – I think she had given up on my hare-brained business schemes long before. To give her credit, Rose did have a particular reason to be more concerned than usual as she was pregnant with our second child. In her usual phlegmatic style, I suppose she took the view that me being out of the way was at least one less child to get under her feet!

We were now living in Epping, and I found a suitable site in the High Street and set about having it fitted out the way I wanted as a dedicated card shop. There was no blueprint to follow, because nothing like this had ever been attempted before. However, I was fortunate to have a close friend, Roy Peppiatt, who was a shop fitter, and he came to my rescue, setting about the place with a couple of men, attaching display panels to the walls and erecting card racks supplied by *Hallmark* in the middle of the shop.

When we had finished and the cards were placed in the racks, I must admit to feeling well satisfied, although the greater feeling was tiredness because we were in the small hours of the morning and I wanted to be back in the shop by 7 o'clock to prepare for my first day trading as *Clinton Cards*.

Choosing the name 'Clinton Cards' seemed obvious to me as I liked the alliteration. I didn't spend ages deliberating over the name – it just came into my head and I knew that is what it would be. Subconsciously, by including my son's name, I may have had hopes that one day there might be something substantial enough for him to want to take over, but that's probably overstating the case. I needed a name for the shop, I liked the name *Clinton Cards* and that's all there was to it.

It actually seemed a bit scary standing in the shop with acres of space for cards. What if nobody came in – would I become bankrupt? All my instincts told me not, but I must admit to feeling a little apprehensive about all that space. I only hoped it would fill up with customers… if only out of curiosity. Of course, I had no idea then what it might lead to, but it was pretty special nonetheless as I locked the doors at 3.00 am and made my weary way home.

I was also feeling special for another reason, and there is no way I'll ever be able to forget the exact date I opened my first card shop. It was 17th April 1968… because our daughter Deborah, or Debbie as she soon became known, was born the day before – not my best piece of timing in the world, but good old Rose was very understanding given the circumstances, and thankfully this was before the modern trend of fathers being present at the birth. The further away the husband was the better, was the opinion of most women… he had done enough already!

There was no fanfare that morning when I opened the doors of a *Clinton Cards* shop for the first time – why should there be, it was just another shop in the high street – so I just got on with serving the customers. In passing, I asked what they thought of the shop. In a typically British non-committal way I was told that it was 'nice' or 'OK', but in my own mind I knew that it was better than 'nice' and 'OK'. Some were a bit more effusive about how much range we stocked and how the cards were 'easy to see' on the racks rather than being bundled together in a box to be sorted through. And, amazingly, I don't think one person mentioned the prices!

I was also visited by other traders in the High Street, most of them doom-mongers predicting my demise. How could a shop selling only cards survive? Their views were only strengthened when they saw what I was selling giftwrap paper for. Newsagents were selling it for a penny a sheet, and here was me charging fourpence. Surely I was off my head! They gave me six months at best... and here was me having signed up for a 20-year lease.

A memorable moment came a few days later when Rose popped into the shop with Clinton and our newborn daughter, Debbie. Clinton could not quite make out why his name was on the front fascia and asked was it his shop... he and others have been asking the same question ever since!

Business was encouraging to start with, nothing special but enough to suggest I was on the right track. As with cards in newsagents, it was noticeable that the majority of customers were women. It would appear that buying cards for the family must be somewhere in the wife's marriage vows. In my experience most men only seem to enter a card shop three or four times a year: Valentine's Day, Mother's Day, for the birthday of their partner and, for the more enlightened chaps, Christmas as well.

Something which gave me great satisfaction and proved once and for all that my instincts had been right was that first Christmas Eve in my very first *Clinton Cards* shop – we sold over 200 padded boxed cards... and I still had a few left for good measure! Despite having a staff of three – Vesta, Doris and Ann – we were all kept busy and prospects for the future looked promising.

This first shop was 18 x 60ft, with a small storeroom behind. It seemed massive to start with, but as time progressed I realised that this was not excessive, particularly when I started to increase the range of goods sold to include what is now known as 'plush' in the trade – soft toys, balloons, paraphernalia for birthday parties, and even a few pictures, often with a royal theme.

Over the next three or four years business continued to grow and I opened another five card shops, taking over premises which included a gift shop, a grocer's and a baker's – as long as it was in a good location, its previous incarnation did not matter.

Another opportunity came my way, which was too good to miss. I was in a newsagents chatting to one of my regulars one day when she mentioned that she and her sister were selling up and she asked if I might be interested in buying the place. After a long discussion I ended up making her an offer and I found myself the proud (if misguided) owner of a newsagents! Was I mad or what!

The shop had an extensive range of daily papers, although it did not sell evening papers or Sundays. In addition, the shop sold magazines, stationery and cards... with more cards in the pipeline! It also did a good line in annuals. It was a strange set-up because, actually, I had bought two shops, the second being a sweet shop and tobacconist. However, they were not next to each other – there was another shop in between – so I couldn't join them together and save on staffing costs... but at least I could sell greeting cards in each shop!

I had agreed to keep on the chap who marked up the papers and looked after the paperboys. However, tragically, within weeks he died, a terribly sad event for all concerned, especially as he was only in his fifties. As it took several weeks for me to find a new manager, I now had to be at the shop at 4.00 am to mark up the papers and oversee deliveries for ten paperboys… who needs sleep anyway!

The newsagents was a sound business, but selling so many different lines of stock only confirmed my thoughts that specialising was the way ahead. What's more, I made far more from the cards than from the combined sweet shop and newsagents… and it was less hassle.

I wouldn't like to call it a mid-life crisis, but as my 40th birthday approached I began to wonder about how long I wanted to continue running the shops. I had eight of them, and whilst business was good I started to think that I should perhaps slow down. By now we had moved seven times and were living in a nice detached house, which we owned outright. Money was not a problem, particularly if I sold my assets, and doing so would allow me to achieve my ambition of owning a *Rolls Royce*. To cut a long story short, this is exactly what I did. At the ripe old age of 39 I decided to retire – well, if not retire, then perhaps take it easy for a few months as I had worked myself to a standstill.

I sold seven of the eight shops, three to the chain of newsagents, *Martins*, but I did keep the card shop in Hoddesdon for posterity. I made it a condition of sale that I would keep the name 'Clinton Cards', but we had a £2,000 difference of opinion over the valuation of the shops. As this was becoming a stumbling block we tossed a coin… thankfully I won! My adversary took it in good heart and said to me, "Something to tell the grandchildren!" I paid the money into my bank account on my 40th birthday. Happy Birthday to me!

Tel

Mean and moody aged 14

With Mum and Tel

With Dad

Private 22581671, just gone in and just come out

The Big Day for Rose and me, 19th December 1953

Ricky outside our first house in Ilford   Earning a bit of extra money decorating...

...to pay for Clinton's new pram

Happy days with the children growing up

Dad and his lad sharing a passion for cars

My first venture into the retail trade...
... I was always looking to clean up!

Epping - my very first card shop

Yet another retailing idea

Serving in the newsagents

Getting a taste for the finer things in life... love the jacket, Clinton!

Our special card to celebrate the Queen's 60th Birthday

...and the Queen Mother's 100th Birthday

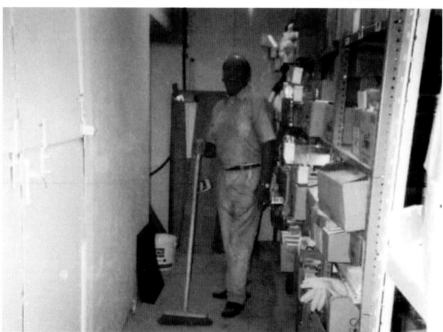

Up against the clock opening another shop

Celebrating the shop opening

With Clinton outside our new Head Office in 1984

Finally being graced by a visit from Ray Cottington

He's not such a bad lad!

Clinton and Debbie celebrating Mother's Day with their Mum

A trip down memory lane with brother Alan

Ann Copping who was at our
first shop in Epping...

...and still with Clintons 25 years later.

Celebrating the first 25 years
of Clinton Cards

Terry Venables signing a game called 'The Manager'

Celebrating St George's Day

I had made it and I owned my very own *Rolls Royce*, so what now? At this time *Rolls Royces* were like gold dust. If you ordered one you had to wait months, and some people were even buying them and selling them on at a premium. With such demand and a reasonable track record in selling, I decided to see if I could make a few bob being a car dealer... albeit a very posh car dealer. I did quite well at this, selling four *Rollers* in one week alone, but then came the fuel crisis of 1972, and with it petrol rationing... having survived a war, here we were back on petrol coupons.

Well, as anyone knows, *Rolls Royces* are not bought for their fuel economy, and with petrol being so hard to come by demand for these luxury cars disappeared overnight. It was back to the drawing board for me.

It was at about this time that I started to feel unwell. I said to my doctor, "I get pains in my chest when I do that," pressing my chest to demonstrate. His response was, "Well don't do that!" This was well before such gags by Tommy Cooper – trust me to have a comedian for a doctor! He prescribed tranquillisers, but went on to give me some good advice. "Don," he said, "you need to work. You're the sort of bloke who can't take it easy. Continue like this and you'll be dead in six months." Thanks Doc!

Oh well, I suppose I'd better get back into selling cards... but this time I'll do it differently... I'll see just how far I can go...

5 | If a Job's Worth Doing...

So now it was a case of starting all over again, but doing it properly this time. I had proved that specialist greeting card shops were viable; it was now just a case of multiplying the concept before other companies got into the market.

As I had discovered all those years earlier when reading about the so-called self-made millionaires in the *Sunday Pictorial*, success breeds success. It is easier to do things on a big scale – if you have serious money and backing you can expand rapidly. I was not in this enviable position. Sure, I had a few bob, but for the next few years I was going to have to keep my head down, work hard and try to build slowly, from one shop to two, from two shops to three and so on. In some ways the biggest step was from one shop to two, because this represented a 100% increase – from two to three shops was only 50%.

Not only did a second shop necessitate taking on extra staff, but it made cover more of a problem. When there was just one shop I could always take over whenever needed. It might have taken me away from some other job, but nothing was more important than the shops and face-to-face dealings with customers. Good staff are always a must – anything else can wait. With more shops, I had Vesta to cover any unexpected staff absences, but it was a gamble that two people would not be off at the same time. Out of necessity there were times when there were only two members of staff in a shop – again, not an ideal situation, but it was the way it had to be when setting out. It also relied heavily on goodwill. For example, if there were only two people in the shop, lunchtimes were non-existent and even popping out to the loo had to be carefully timed between customers. This might have been acceptable for short periods, particularly as the occasional bonus in the pay packet at the end of the week went a long way, but it was not a viable way to run a business in the long term. Health and safety legislation makes this a non-starter today, but fortunately the red tape was not quite as restrictive in the early years.

I also had to be careful not to spend too much time in the shops myself if I was ever going to make any money – the only way I was going to do that was to employ others to work for me, although I could never expect others to work as hard as me… after all, it was my company. I was in a bit of a dilemma – the old adage of having to speculate to accumulate.

I was fortunate that Clinton was 12 or 13, an age when he could help out from time to time. What better Saturday job than helping out in his old man's shop… and it saved me having to pay pocket money. Seriously, though, I have always felt that you only appreciate things if you have to work for them, and I am pleased to say that Clinton never shied away from the family work ethic. He helped out whenever he could, and thought nothing of working ridiculously long hours… a real chip off the old block. I've always wondered whether it helped that his name was synonymous with the shop… a benefit or a millstone round his neck? You'll have to wait until he writes his own book to find out.

For the next few years it was a case of growing one shop at a time. When I had built up enough capital to start another shop I would have a word with the bank manager, negotiate the lease and start all over again. I knew the East London and Essex areas like the back of my hand from my days driving around selling cards out of the back of my car. I kept a mental note of thriving areas and potential shops, so when I was ready it was just a case of seeing what was available at the time.

After that, all I had to do was refurbish the shop in the *Clinton Cards* style and employ the right people. This might sound easy but it was very time-consuming, especially as I was wearing lots of other hats at the same time. I would ensure that I visited each shop at least once a week, usually daily in the early stages, or later on phoning to ascertain that everything was running all right and monitoring the level of sales.

Being a hands-on character, I wanted to know what was happening in each of my shops. I don't like surprises, and there's no need for them if you set things up properly following a proven formula. In the early days it was easy to monitor everything, but this was less so as things grew. Even now, when there are shops I have never even been into, I make a point of visiting new areas from time to time. It used to be every Saturday, but I'm beginning to slow down a bit now. I decide on a part of the country and visit several shops in the area. The first unsuspecting soul has the biggest shock when I turn up because after that the bush telegraph gets going. Also, poor Rose knows that whenever we are in the car together, I cannot pass through a town where there is one of our shops... and that is most towns!

In the mid-1970s there was competition from the likes of *Hallmark* and *American Greetings* from the United States, but we tended to stick to our own parts of the country and there was plenty of room for all of us. In a way we helped each other, in that the more the public saw specialist card shops, the more they became familiar with the concept – we were all helping to educate the marketplace. In fact, I found that it usually took two or three years for a shop to become established in the high street and achieve its optimal level of sales, especially in the early years when dedicated card shops were still a bit of a novelty.

A bigger threat was the established high street chains. Even in 1988 when *Clinton Cards* was floated on the Unlisted Securities Market, we still only had 3% of the UK market. I knew that we offered a far more extensive range of greeting cards, but customers like convenience and if they were in *WH Smith's* and could find a suitable card, why go elsewhere?

This gave me two obstacles to overcome. The first was to educate shoppers to the fact that *Clinton Cards* provided the best range and quality, so if they were looking for two or three cards they would want to come to my shops. The second factor was to ensure that my shops were convenient. A customer might be prepared to walk an extra hundred yards or so to go to the better shop, but they would be less prepared to walk to the other end of the high street. Therefore, in the larger towns, if necessary I would have to consider having two shops. This was something totally unheard of, but I achieved this first in Cambridge. It caused a bit of a stir initially and people thought I was mad. But I had come across such reservations before, and as long as the figures stacked up, I was the one who was laughing. What's more, anything that had people talking about *Clinton Cards* shops was OK by me. Who was it who said, 'There's no such thing as bad publicity?'

There was no shortage of ideas I wanted to implement, but for the time being it was a case of growing slowly, one at a time. And for this there was plenty of scope in my neck of the woods, so there was no need to get too big for my boots.

I have been asked if I had a business plan in these early years. Today, thanks to being a publicly quoted company, we have to have mission statements, goals, business plans and what have you. Back then it was more a case of me thinking, 'Wouldn't it be great to have a few more shops by the end of the year,' or perhaps, 'Twenty-five shops in three years would be good.' Call it fag-packet economics, but it seemed to work. As I've said many times before, business is common sense and budgeting, any housewife will tell you that. Indeed, one housewife who eventually lived in a house with a posh black front door with a Bobby on her doorstep was also known to advocate this view in the late 1970s and onwards.

There are now university degree courses which study shop selection, 'footfall', and other trendy terms. To my mind it is common sense. Show me any high street and within two minutes I'll tell you where I want one of my shops located. It's a combination of pavement size, traffic flows, parking, bus stops, and, significantly, proximity to the other key shops. Being next-door to *Marks and Spencer* is always a winner, and in the early days landlords were not always as sharp as they are now. Due to our success it is acknowledged in the industry that *Clinton Cards* is a benchmark against which other rents are set, partly because of the sites we demand. I suppose it is a compliment of sorts, but certainly a backhanded one as far as I am concerned – let the landlords do their own research not piggyback off me! Sermon over.

Over the years I became responsible for introducing terms common to the greeting card industry and to other industries for that matter. Take 'frozen credit' as a case in point. As I have said earlier, one of the conversations which gave me nightmares in the early years when selling cards to newsagents was the chap who was so delighted because he had sold out of Christmas cards two weeks before Christmas. What a waste. I was adamant that I never wanted to sell out of any line. If I sold out it meant that I had not ordered enough stock in the first place. The customer might then go elsewhere and I had lost a sale. It also meant that the customer might not come back another time and I would never realise the shop's potential.

I promised myself that my shops would hold a reasonable level of stock in the first place and have storage for a small margin of back-up stock. I also needed an efficient reordering system. This became easier with size as I then had more clout with suppliers. There are suppliers who will testify to me threatening to withdraw the whole account if certain stock was not delivered to a certain place by a certain time. I am sure I was not popular, but popularity is not always the highest priority in business.

The danger of ensuring you hold enough stock is that there is likely to be some left over. I can see that a case can be made for selling off Christmas cards in the New Year, but I have never been a fan of sales. A sale implies that you have overcharged the customer in the first place. If a box of cards is worth £2.99 on 23rd December, how come it is worth half that a week later? Either it is worth the money or not and I did not want to insult my customers in this way. Where stock levels are so high that storage costs become significant, I have sometimes had to bite my tongue and renounce these principles, but I don't like it – surely there had to be a better way?

As our buying clout increased we moved on to sale or return – we only paid for what we sold, the rest was returned to the supplier. There was a grey area over shop-soiled stock – cards with bent corners etc – but I always enjoyed haggling over these! The question was what to do with annual cards like Mother's Day, Valentine's Day, Easter, etc where there was no demand until the following year. In the usual course of events these would be returned to the supplier until the next year, whereupon they would be wheeled out again. This took time and effort, but as we had reasonable areas for storage, I suggested an alternative, 'frozen credit'. Effectively, we would hold the stock until the following year and pay for what was sold then. I suggested this to a couple of suppliers who were happy to give it a try. As we always paid our invoices on time and were totally trustworthy, they had nothing to lose. They tried it, liked it, and now frozen credit is an established part of the industry, and some other seasonal industries as well.

Dealing fairly with suppliers has always been important to me – I suppose it goes back to my days hawking cards and expecting payment with delivery. It is not only a matter of respect; it makes good business sense too. No contract can be one-sided. If it is there comes a time when the supplier will say, "Enough is enough – I don't care how important you are to us, we cannot continue to operate this way." Additionally, it is difficult to make other demands, or call in favours regarding extra stock in double-quick time to help you out of a hole if goodwill has been lost. I am all for tough negotiating, but once the negotiations are over, play fair.

Over the past 40 years it is interesting how card styles have changed. Whilst there are more blank cards for people to write their own messages inside, there are still plenty of people who like to buy cards with poems and heartfelt sentiments. Embossed cards seem to come in and out of fashion with a heartening regularity, and there has been a huge advance in recent years for artistic cards with original and interesting additions, like quilling and découpàge. These three-dimensional cards give a feel of being handmade, which they are to an extent because they require individual attention as opposed to coming straight off a printing press. As a result the cards cost a lot more, but people are prepared to pay for quality, especially for a special friend or loved one.

Cards depicting the old masters have always been popular, with the impressionists and tasteful art also being in good demand; however, the bestsellers over the years have been pictures of dogs or horses, closely followed by cats. We must have sold thousands of different styles, yet the appetite never seems to diminish. There has been a rise in musical and gimmicky cards with advances in technology, and a current appetite for 'celebrity' cards, but I suppose the greatest changes in style have been the humorous cards. We went through a phase of the very popular *Gordon Fraser* cards but now there appears to be no limit as to what is available, although I always insist that we stock nothing which I perceive to be bad taste. Call me old-fashioned, but my methods are tried and tested, and whilst I'm keen to encourage initiative, freshen up our offerings and hopefully be open to good ideas, I tend to fall back on the old adage, 'If it ain't broke, don't fix it.'

I am also a stickler for having the right feel for the shop – or 'ambience' as the marketing people prefer to call it. Again it comes down to common sense. Choosing a card is not always easy, and some people take an eternity to make precisely the right choice. The shop therefore has to be conducive for musing over decisions, an enjoyable place to be. This involves good lighting, plenty of space to stand without being in the way of others, quality carpets and scrupulous cleanliness. We might not have got to the stage of offering tea and coffee as we'd rather customers not spend all day choosing one card, but short of that I want the shops to be as pleasurable as possible.

A huge factor regarding the feel of any shop is music, a subject very dear to my heart. It must never be obtrusive, but gentle background 'feel-good' music. Managers of all our shops are only allowed to play a range of CDs which we oversee, and we are also specific about the sound level. Nothing can be left to chance.

Over the years I have been in hundreds of cards shops run by competitors – I have no problem with this as I know that any competitor worth their salt will have been in plenty of our shops to see how we operate. Sometimes I am impressed, other times less so. I have picked up the occasional useful idea, but it is easier to spot things that are wrong rather than what is right. A well laid out and professionally run shop will probably make little impact on a shopper, and rightly so – when looking to buy a card the customer does not want to analyse every detail... that can be left to sad people like me. What the customer will be aware of, however, is if anything isn't to their liking: perhaps the floor is dirty or there's been a spillage which hasn't been cleaned up; messy or poorly stocked displays; the aforementioned noisy music; perhaps some boxes left in the corner; staff chatting to each other unconcerned about a customer request; or, my pet hate, a member of staff chatting away on a mobile phone while serving at the checkout. To me this is the height of rudeness and I am happy to go on record here and say that I would like to hear from anyone who experiences such unprofessional service in any of my shops.

All these things colour a customer's opinion about a shop, if only subconsciously. However, it is this same subconscious which might lead the customer to pass by a *Clinton Cards* shop next time and buy from a competitor. Naturally, with all the hard work we invest in trying to get things right, anything within our control which loses us a customer makes my blood boil.

One competitor I came across early on didn't have a clue. His shop was at the wrong end of Ilford High Street and he was trying to sell discounted cards. He was offering five cards for one pound, so his customers were looking for the biggest cards they could find. I actually stood there and timed how long people were in his shop. Some were there for 30 minutes or more to select their five special cards, and as the shop wasn't very big in the first place this was preventing other people looking at the displays. In fact, many of them were coming along to our shop where they could get what they wanted in a timely manner.

The other problem with his way of trading was that overheads still had to be paid. I know that the price of cards can be a common complaint, but to provide a wide choice of high quality cards in pleasant surroundings costs money. He discovered this the hard way, by going out of business, which certainly didn't help any of his customers. Ultimately, people make decisions based on value for money and, as we have been known to sell a card or two over the years, I like to think we've got something right.

Additionally, the quality of cards sold in these discount shops was questionable to say the least. I am insistent that all our cards are top-notch because any inferior or cheap-looking cards will taint the rest of what is being offered. I want customers to know that we only sell the best quality cards, so I started using the phrase, 'When only the best is good enough'. And to emphasise the point, the word *Best* was in a different style.

To further distinguish *Clinton Cards* from other shops which came and went on the high street, I decided that a common theme was needed – a standard colour and style of shop window. I wanted a colour that would stand out, and on looking round I realised that no other shop fascias were orange, so orange it became and orange it has been ever since. My hope was that if customers were impressed with our shops they would recognise other branches and make a bee-line to them. I also hoped that people would start talking about *Clinton Cards*, because there is no better recommendation than word of mouth.

Marketing as we know it today was still in its infancy, but bit by bit I was moving in the right direction. To help in all this I thought that a slogan would be useful as it could be a feature of the shop window, be included in all displays and even be printed on our bags. It may sound pretty mundane now, but at the time it was cutting-edge stuff. All this was fine and dandy, but what should the slogan be? In the end I came up with, 'Think of a card... Think of Clintons'. This is now in every shop window and in the rear window of all of our cars and vans.

In these early years it was just a case of sticking to what I knew and trying to replicate it when I had the opportunity, borrowing more money when the bank manager felt that increased sales from the current shops justified it. In this I was fortunate to have a bank manager who believed in me. Mr Stevens from *Midland Bank* was a man I could do business with. He was from the old school and was prepared to go out on a limb to support me as he could see that the business was solid, and he would help me ride out minor cashflow inconveniences. This was at a time when bank managers could make their own decisions without having to refer to an area or regional office and to some spotty graduate with no experience of the real world, let alone the business world. He used to call me 'Son' and talk to me like my dad never did.

Mr Stevens had learned banking the old way and as long as I was within his limits would give me pretty well what I liked as he knew I would always be good for the money in the long run. I have provided various personal guarantees, even mortgaging the house, so the bank was not too exposed, but it still helped to have an understanding manager. Indeed, when Mr Stevens was promoted to a bigger branch, I moved my account to stay with him. A bank manager who understands your business and, more importantly, knows you, is worth his weight in gold. A simple phone call can save all sorts of hassle of filling in business plans and cashflow forecasts. We all like to deal with people we know and trust. I just wish the banks would take note of this and not persist in anonymous business centres where the staff change every five minutes.

I was doing well, the business was moving in the right direction and I was driving a nice car. In fact, I was rather proud of the car so I was none too impressed when a chap on a motorbike, who wasn't looking where he was going, went into the back of me. There wasn't too much damage, but enough to cost a few quid to fix, so I was not too polite. To his credit, he accepted the blame and couldn't do enough to sort things out. He only lived a few roads away so he asked me to follow him back to his house so that he could give me some money to fix my car. I went with him as I certainly didn't want to be out of pocket.

The man only had a modest upstairs flat, but he asked me in and offered me a cup of tea while he got some money together. His wife and small baby were also there and she spoke to me while he was getting the money. I was feeling pretty uncomfortable by this time, especially when he came back into the room with a tea caddy where they obviously kept any hard-earned savings they'd been able to put by, just like my dear old mum had done. It was then that I realised what a total pratt I was being. Here was me with enough money to fix the car without noticing, and here was this well-meaning man trying to do all he could, even though it would cost him dear. I may have had everything in material terms, yet he had so much more. I stood up, told him to keep his money and not worry about the accident. That man taught me a very valuable lesson, and if ever I feel

I am getting too big for my boots I try to remember him and what he taught me that day.

In 1977 when Clinton left school at 16, he came to work for me. Even if he was a bit wet behind the ears, he was a fast learner, and he was certainly not frightened of hard work or long hours, and that goes a long way in my book. It was interesting (Rose may claim I used other words) working with Clinton because he questioned many of my decisions. Don't get me wrong, this was good because it showed initiative and it is a good way to learn, but I found it strange having to justify myself to someone else – after all, I'd been doing things pretty much the way I wanted for years and here I was having to justify myself to a teenager.

If I found working with Clinton a strain at times, I know that it must have been a hundred times worse for him. Having a dad who always thinks he is right (because I am) cannot be easy and it must have been tempting for Clinton to tell me where to get off. We had several bust-ups over the years, but we were both big enough to come back the next day, clear the air and move on.

These bust-ups were usually over some small point like the design of a display, but in many ways I saw this as positive. It was because we both cared and had a passion for the business. I would far prefer these passionate differences of opinion than have some tame 'yes man' who doesn't give a fig for his job. Like me, Clinton lives and breathes greeting cards, and I like to think this has been reflected in the growth of the company.

Another important member to join *Clinton Cards* in 1977 was John Preston, who had been a friend for years. John, an electrician by trade, worked for his brother-in-law, a property developer, but when the business fell on hard times John was made redundant. I saw a future for John in my business as he could turn his hand to most things – in fact, John was the first director of *Clinton Cards*, staying with me until he retired after 30 years' service.

I like to write poems on special occasions and John's retirement was just that, so I include his tribute here:

Dear John

I thought that I would write
A farewell verse for you;
After thirty years with Clint and I,
It's the least that I could do.

You have been with me, right from the start
Of *Clinton Cards* Mark Two,
Mark One was when I really struggled;
I wish you had been there too.

But now here we are with all those years
Behind us; where did they go?
We worked so hard and enjoyed it all,
Through sunshine, rain and snow.

To look back on all those years,
I sometimes wish we did it later;
But then I think of what was achieved,
A household name – what's greater!

You and I were young men then;
The laughs were in abundance.
We clowned around and joked a lot;
Not a thought of redundance.

I will miss you very much,
And so will many more;
I find it strange to retire at sixty-five,
When you could have stayed to eighty-four.

Still, I just have to say,
Good luck to you and your new start;
I wish you all you wish yourself,
And that comes right from the heart.

P.S.
If you change your mind, I'll see you on Monday!

Another person who came to see me about a job was John Cutts; his daughter Debbie was a shop manager and I always welcome personal recommendations. I had an office at home with wood panelled walls and a couple of very nice yew chairs – they cost a bob or two but they really set the place off and gave it a bit of class. I interviewed John there, but it could not have got off to a worse start. John appeared to be quite relaxed, almost too relaxed, because he leaned back so far that he tipped right over, ending up with his legs in the air, breaking this beautiful chair in the process. Talk about an embarrassing way to start an interview! All we could do was laugh, the ice was broken and John ended up with the job, working with us for many years. In fact, looking back, I wonder if this was a ploy to make me feel embarrassed for him. All I can say is that if it was, it certainly worked – good on you, John.

During these years I had been able to experiment with the range of cards we offered, increasing this substantially as I always wanted *Clinton Cards* to be at the forefront of the market, giving more choice to our customers. They seemed to like what we offered, and so I was keen to increase the range further. Suppliers enjoyed our product meetings because it gave their designers scope to test their creativity. They soon got to know my tastes and I was not hesitant in giving my opinions. I also enjoyed making suggestions and between us the range continued to broaden.

Having a feel for what customers want, I would often request cards that the suppliers were not too keen to produce. One example was a range of large, high quality, gift boxed, satin-padded, musical 18th and 21st birthday cards. The supplier told me that to make these would require a price tag of £12 per card. I told them to go ahead and that I would underwrite their costs – for good measure I instructed them to add a corner strip with the words 'Exclusive to Clintons'. If I was going to take the risk I wanted to ensure we got the benefit of exclusivity. This was back in 1984, and the cards sold like hot cakes, despite the seemingly high price. You cannot put a price on sentiment, added to which customers are discerning when it comes to quality and value for money.

By this time we had built a small but growing reputation within the industry, which made it easier to have arrangements with the main suppliers. We dealt with such publishers as *Valentines of Dundee, CAG, Rust Craft, Fine Art* and *Royle*. However, the dominant suppliers by far were the American-owned *Hallmark* and

American Greetings. I particularly admired *Hallmark* at that time because they exuded quality, something I have always advocated myself. I actually bought one of my first shops from *Hallmark*, who dabbled in the retail trade in the early years, and it was a great day in 1994 when I actually bought the UK arm of *Hallmark* to become the largest independent greeting card retailer in the world... however, I am getting a little ahead of myself here. There are a few rather interesting steps to record before we get to that stage in the story.

In 1981 we opened our tenth shop, surpassing the number of premises (including laundrettes) I'd had before I 'retired'. It had been a long haul, but we now had the building blocks in place to look to the future.

6 | Going Public

1984 was a big year in the history of *Clinton Cards*. It was the year we moved to our head office in Loughton. Head office sounds rather grand. It might be a bit more posh now, but back in 1984 it wasn't anything to write home about. It was basically a 10,000 sq ft warehouse with some office space attached. To put that in context, we now have a store in Bath which is bigger. That having been said, we were delighted with it at the time and it was another stepping stone in our progress. And, what's more, it was a significant step up from the room above our shop in Chingford which had sufficed very adequately as a head office for the past ten years.

This year, 1984, was also a year that saw unparalleled growth. By December we had 22 shops and we were opening one a month. In the past couple of decades things have moved on even more, but to provide an idea of what we were offering at this time I shall describe the formula I was advocating in each of the new shops.

Most stores were in excess of 1,500 sq ft, with at least 70% of the display devoted to cards – *Hallmark* supplied around 30% of our cards at this time. The rest of the space was given over to giftwrap and dressings, wedding and special occasion keepsakes, promotions, stationery and soft toy products. We also had a range of exclusive products, like party novelties, gift stationery and what we called 'social stationery' – invitations, pre-printed acceptance cards etc.

In 1984 each branch had a 12-16ft display of 'good luck' keys and horseshoes, and boxed cards. Also, no shop had less than 12ft of giftwrap, which was sold flat, rolled and folded to suit all preferences, and there would also be a comprehensive selection of ribbons, bows and tags. Over more recent years presentation bags and boxes can be added to this list.

When it came to 'plush' (soft toys etc), in the early 1980s *Garfield* was all the rage. We like to keep abreast of changes in taste and over the years have offered *Peanuts* (especially *Snoopy*), *South Park*, *Teletubbies* and *The Simpsons* to name a few. Such characters were ideal as they could be suspended from the ceiling, providing an attractive display as well as saving space which could be utilised by other lines... what a happy man this made me!

However, not everything went smoothly. In the early 1980s we signed a deal to sell merchandise from the film, ET, as all reports predicted a huge box office hit. The film was a hit, sensationally so; the only problem was that the merchandise did not arrive in time and we lost a substantial amount of money. All we could do was put it down to experience and ensure that in future any such agreement was subject to strict delivery dates.

Displays were changed regularly to maintain interest and freshness, but change would be necessary anyway to accommodate special occasions like Valentine's Day, Easter, Mother's Day etc, with a particularly large effort being made at Christmas. Each shop manager knew what displays had to appear at what time, and the associated music... nothing was left to chance.

A typical shop frontage was relatively small at perhaps 18ft, but it might stretch back over a hundred feet. This reflects many of the established high streets – when it comes to dedicated retail outlets and shopping centres, the frontage is usually larger... and the rents more than proportionately so!

The final part of our offering was for attractive, colourful displays with interest at every level, and the aforementioned tasteful relaxing music in the background. So there you have it, the perfect formula to set up in competition... but that was in 1984 and things have moved on a bit since then!

Clinton and I used to pop over to the United States occasionally because at this time they were in the forefront of ideas when it came to greeting cards and other goods relevant to our shops. That is not to say we were seduced by all things American. Our customers are very discerning, and just because a product sells in America does not mean the same will be true here. American tastes are different and it was our job to spot what would migrate well and what wouldn't.

Going to America with Clinton in 1983 had additional benefits. Being upgraded to first class is always a bonus, but it was here that we met John Condon who was also flying out on the buyers' trip to *Hallmark Cards* in Kansas City. He had been working for *Martin the Newsagent* for the best part of 25 years, so we had plenty to chat about. I was impressed by John's knowledge of the greeting card industry and I was in my element discussing the minutiae of the business, not least because I had never met anyone before with a similar encyclopaedic knowledge of this specialist area.

THINK OF A CARD...

John had got into the greeting card industry by accident, having planned on joining *Glaxo* in 1958. However, it transpired that he was a year too young and they told him to go away and do something else, returning when he had a bit more experience. This was their mistake because that year he worked as a rep for the greeting card and stationery wholesaler, *PG Hicks*, owned by Bernard Martin, managing director of the *Martin Retail Group*. By the end of the year John was earning too much money to want to join *Glaxo*. He continued to work hard and ten years later was in charge of merchandising and buying, which was when he began to consider greeting cards as a significant business in its own right.

During the trip to Kansas I was so impressed with John that I said to him, "One day, when we're big enough, I'll give you a job." Playing me at my own game he replied, "One day, when I'm big enough, I'll accept it." Two years later he was big enough and he joined *Clinton Cards* as marketing director. This might have been his official job title, but as I needed some area managers at the time, I asked him to appoint these. So he effectively became operations director as well for a while. Delegation may not have been my strong point at the time, but John proved to me that when you employ capable people it is best to let them get on with the job in hand, and over the years he has proved his worth time and time again.

John was always the perfect gentleman, but I think he was a bit surprised by our work ethic – like everyone else, he was expected to work Saturdays... not just occasionally, but *every* Saturday!

One of the first things John did was visit all the branches to meet everyone and get a feel for the *Clinton Cards* way of working. In chatting to the shop managers he asked what they would change if they had a magic wand. Their answer was revealing: "Tell the directors to stop coming round the shops countermanding each other!" Oh well, you couldn't blame us for our enthusiasm!

My favourite time for visiting stores was on a Saturday, selecting an area I hadn't been to for a while. My brother Alan invariably came with me, which gave me a chance to bounce ideas around as we drove along. On one of these Saturday jaunts the high street was busy so I parked round the back of the *Clinton Cards* shop and knocked on the back door. I said who I was and asked to be let in, but the manager requested some ID. As I have never carried such a thing I repeated who I was and asked her to open the door. She replied, "I don't care who you are. Unless you have some identification, I'm not letting you in." Alan found this highly amusing, although I can't remember sharing his sense of humour at the time. However, I can laugh at this now and I applaud her for her actions. She was right and I was wrong. There you have it, in writing, me admitting that I was wrong – you'd better frame this page!

I have been fortunate over the years in finding so many loyal and conscientious people, and when I can I like to give them a treat to let them know they are valued. In the early days this might mean taking some cakes into the shop, or perhaps asking the manager to take everyone out for a meal and sending me the bill.

At Christmas I always liked to do something special, which was much easier when we only had a few shops. I used to put some bottles of wine in the car and Alan and I would visit all the shops in turn. When we had too many shops for this to be possible, I would phone each of the shop managers to wish them and their staff Happy

Christmas. One year, when we had more than 50 shops, I lost my voice and so Valerie, my PA, passed on the message while I sat next to her to croak what I could down the phone. Now that we have a more substantial head office, Valerie takes round drinks and mince pies on Christmas Eve.

One Christmas Eve I popped into one of our Epping shops to wish the staff Happy Christmas when the trouser pocket of my lovely mohair suit caught on a drawer handle, pulling the trousers apart down the seam of the leg. There I was standing in my underpants amidst a lot of Ho Ho Hoing from staff and customers alike. I just stood there totally embarrassed, before seeing the funny side of it and laughing along with the rest of them. In fact, I seem to recall getting into the spirit of it and doing a hula-hula dance for good measure. I'd lost all dignity already, so what the heck! Thankfully, the shop manager, Ann Copping, came to the rescue with a handful of safety pins, and she proceeded to pin me up so I could continue on my way... a Christmas I'll never forget!

I don't know what it was about me and Epping, but another of our three shops there was the scene of a further mishap when I walked straight into the door, giving my head the most almighty whack. The plate glass door was so clean that I didn't see it – I just assumed the door was open. It made one hell of a noise, which was not surprising given how much my head hurt. Everyone in the shop turned and stared at me, so I just had to shrug it off and pretend that I was OK, holding myself together as best I could. Again it was Ann who was there and she sensed that all was not right because she quickly lifted the counter flap for me to pass through to the storeroom at the back. Once there, out of sight of the customers, I dropped to my haunches and held my head in my hands, thinking it was about to explode. So you see, stickers on the door are not just to advertise our wares, they're to stop the likes of me from bashing my bonce!

As far back as 1986 I had set my sights on the Unlisted Securities Market (USM), the junior market of the London Stock Exchange. To be honest, I actually had my sights set on the Stock Exchange proper, but you have to start somewhere. Releasing some cash in this way would make it easier to lease premises and therefore help with our further expansion plans.

By 1988 we had 77 shops, having grown from 22 in 1984, with shops extending from the south coast up into Oxfordshire, and from Bath in the West to Norwich in the East.

I had been using the solicitors *Romain, Coleman and Co* in Walthamstow for years when buying property, and by this time I had persuaded John Coleman to join the management team as a non-executive director. John had been a close friend for over 30 years and obviously had a good understanding of the business and my plans for the future. We instructed *Samuel Montagu* and *Price Waterhouse* to act on our behalf, but I found it mind-boggling the amount of indemnities they wanted from me... talk about the shirt off my back! I spent several Sundays checking piles of papers word by word.

The press announcement was released on 20th April 1988, and what better than to quote the article from the premier of all business papers, the *Financial Times*.

USM Prepares Greeting for Clinton Cards

From Billericay to Bognor they buy them in bulk. Greeting cards are big business and *Clinton Cards* means to benefit from the boom. It is joining the Unlisted Securities Market via a placing and offer for sale which will capitalise the company at £20.26m.

Samuel Montagu is placing 2.17m shares with institutions and offering 1.17m for sale, representing 24.7% of the enlarged equity. At the 150p offer price, *Clinton* is valued on an historic P/E of 16.4 on the basis of earnings per share of 9.13p for the year ended January 31 1988.

Mr Don Lewin, chairman and managing director, opened his first shop in Epping 20 years ago, naming it after his son. There are now 77 *Clinton Cards* shops, all in the south east and East Anglia, which last year sold 25m cards. *Hallmark* is the main supplier at 40%.

"Most of our customers are women between 20 and 45," said Mr Lewin. Funny cards are gaining in popularity but the best sellers remain the sentimental ones with long verses. Horses and dogs always go down a treat.

Clinton's cards range from 45p to £30, and for the latter you will get a giant satin padded creation with bows and ribbons that plays a tune. Cards represent 66% of *Clinton's* business, giftwrap 9%, stationery and novelties another 9%, and what the company calls 'plush' the final 16% – soft toys and cartoon character products.

The UK greeting card business is worth about £470m a year, and *Clinton* has a 3% market share. Specialist shops have 25% of the £470m, with the chains such as *WH Smith* holding the balance.

Clinton's policy is to choose prime sites in the high street and quality shopping malls. "I like to be close to *Marks and Spencer*," said Mr Lewin.

The offer and placing will raise £2.6m for the company, to be used for expansion. Don Lewin's aim is to see a *Clinton* shop in every major town in the country.

Comment

Specialist retailers have been having a fairly good time of it recently and *Clinton* could be one to add to the list. Pre-tax profits have risen from £118,000 in 1984 to £1.56m in 1988. Cards are a growth market – people still want to send tangible greetings but they are too lazy to write, hence the boom in both seasonal offerings and 'trivial' cards of the "Hi, I'm just sitting here thinking of you" variety. *Clinton* has a solid record of steady growth, a wealth of experience in its management and the potential – with fresh funds – to grow quickly both organically and through acquisition. The price is not extravagant.

It was the *Daily Express* which explained the implications in more down-to-earth fashion:

> The Lewin family will be worth £15 million on paper when their *Clinton Cards* retail chain comes to the Unlisted Securities Market next week. Don Lewin, his wife and two children – one of whom is also a director – will own 75% of the business when a quarter of the shares are sold in a joint placing and offer-for-sale at 150p each.

* * *

Wow! What I needed now was a strong response to the offer.

I was keen for *Clinton Cards* shares to be bought by the general public, as I felt that our customers should share in any potential rewards. This sentiment was certainly advocated by Mrs Thatcher, who during her time at the helm privatised everything from *British Telecom* and *British Gas*, to the airports, utilities and rail, encouraging tens of thousands of people to own shares for the first time. I knew that there would be more chance of this when news of the offer appeared in *The Sun*.

Profit on the Cards
The Sun, Tuesday, April 26, 1988

> BRITS are a sentimental lot, but they do it with a smile, say retailers *Clinton Cards*.

Clinton, who are offering £5 million worth of shares to the public at 150p each, say we buy more cards than any other country.

The UK card market is worth £500 million and the firm sold 25 million of them last year, the best sellers being funny cards.

Applications must be made through major *Midland Bank* branches by tomorrow morning.

* * *

Preparing for the flotation was both demanding and expensive, but it was a useful discipline in clarifying the way we conducted our business. Until now these were the things I had been deciding on the hoof... my so-called common sense approach. If I am honest, I was quite impressed when I read the formal offer document. I had never read one before, and for anyone in a similar position, I include extracts about our sales and marketing strategy below:

Clinton Cards places particular emphasis on the selection of its shops. They are chosen for the suitability, location and size. Site location, in prominent positions of high pedestrian traffic, is considered to be of paramount importance. In addition, the Group seeks to operate shops that are larger than those of other specialist card retailers and the majority of the shops are between 1,250 and 2,000 sq ft. This enables the merchandise to be displayed in an attractive and prominent manner, thereby encouraging customers to browse and promoting impulse purchasing. Emphasis is placed on lighting and layout. Shop fittings are chosen with care and are continually monitored and replaced as appropriate. The importance of maintaining the appearance of the shops is regularly impressed upon the staff. Directors and area managers visit *Clinton Cards'* shops frequently to ensure that standards of appearance are maintained.

Clinton Cards' shops stock a wide range of cards so as to appeal to a broad customer base drawn from all ages and income groups. The range of cards is continually reviewed. Quality, variety and exclusivity are given high priority and have been enhanced by the introduction of our own brand cards, which are manufactured by a number of existing suppliers and incorporate designs and captions selected by *Clinton Cards.*

Clinton Cards actively seeks to identify new products and is able to assess and respond to customer requirements. In addition to introducing products that reflect current fashions the Group is active in suggesting ideas for new products to suppliers, including ways of expanding the association of a character from cards to other merchandise.

In common with many retail businesses, *Clinton Cards* enjoys high sales in the Christmas period. In each of the last three years, approximately one third of total turnover has been represented by sales in the months of November and December. Whilst *Clinton Cards* seeks to maximise Christmas demand, it has been active in generating sales at other times of the year. This has been achieved through stocking a wide range of non-seasonal products, such as birthdays and many other occasional cards, and also by promoting other times of seasonal demand such as Valentine's Day, Mother's Day, Easter and Father's Day.

Effective management reporting and accounting controls are exercised... The management reporting system provides the directors with sales figures each week and monthly accumulative statistics, both of which are monitored against sales targets for each shop. As the number of shops has increased greater emphasis has been placed on these controls.

* * *

It all sounds pretty impressive... but common sense nonetheless!

Now it was just the little matter of waiting to see how the flotation fared. The next few weeks were a bit of a whirlwind, what with speaking to journalists and producing more and more figures until I could barely see straight, and all the while we had the small matter of running a business.

As it happened, I need not have worried. Despite the share-owning community still feeling somewhat delicate after the effects of Black Monday in October 1987, shares in *Clinton Cards* were 11.3 times oversubscribed.

I will always remember the excitement at the London Stock Exchange on the day of going 'public'. I watched every price fluctuation, knowing that even a penny rise or fall represented thousands of pounds and the culmination for me of so much hard graft over so many years.

At the end of what had been a very good day I purchased some items of memorabilia for friends, relatives and employees to commemorate the day. My embarrassment arose when I was told that they did not accept credit cards – I had to pay in cash. So here I was, just having made millions, having to borrow money from some of my friends! How the mighty fall!

To complete what had already been an amazing year, in November 1988, in Slough, we opened our 100th shop, holding a celebration on the premises to mark this wonderful milestone.

I had many letters of congratulations – plus the odd card or two I'm pleased to report – but I wish to include just one here. It is from the late Derek Black at *Hallmark Cards*, the company so supportive of our business.

HALLMARK CARDS LIMITED
HALLMARK HOUSE · STATION ROAD · HENLEY-ON-THAMES
OXON · RG9 1LQ · TEL: (0491) 578383   TELEX: 847279
FAX NO: (0491) 578817 (GRP. II & III)

10th November 1988

Mr. D. Lewin
Clinton Cards
Crystal Buildings
Debden
Loughton
Essex
1G10 JTH

Dear Don,

Thank you for your kind invitation to join you at Slough
for the opening of your 100th shop. I look forward to
seeing you there for what I hope will be a successful and
memorable day for you.

May I also take this opportunity to congratulate you on
this magnificent achievement.

It does not seem too long ago when we first met and with a
small base of shops you explained your plans for the
future of Clinton Cards.

This 'dream' you have accomplished in a relatively short
time frame. It is a success story without parallel in the
Greeting Card industry and in my opinion stands alongside
the success stories we have seen in other sectors of the
retail trade in the last decade.

I appreciate that for you personally this is an historic
'milestone' but, knowing you, it won't be long before we
are all meeting again to celebrate the next one!

It has been a pleasure to work with you throughout this
period and I would like to add my personal "well done,
Don" to all the deserved accolades you will receive.

yours sincerely

D. H. Black
Sales Director
DHB/HF

DIRECTORS: K.F WHEAL (CHAIRMAN AND CHIEF EXECUTIVE)   L J FARRANT   W.J. STOTT   H.S. BIRTLEY   S A HAMILTON (USA)   R.L STARK (USA)
SECRETARY: L.J FARRANT   REGISTERED OFFICES: HALLMARK HOUSE, STATION ROAD, HENLEY-ON-THAMES, OXON RG9 1LG   REGISTERED IN ENGLAND NO. 1535645   VAT Regn No 363 0932 61

7 | Playing the City Game

The Christmas trading figures were awaited more eagerly than usual in the New Year of 1989 because of the effect City pundits now had on our business. Since the flotation I had got into the habit of checking the share price first thing every morning – not an entirely good idea as it tended to affect my mood. Having the odd share or two myself, a price rise made me even more ebullient than usual, coming up with dozens more ideas, while a sharp dip would see me wanting to work harder or speak to different people to ascertain why sales weren't better.

At this point I feel I must mention Valerie Gumbrell, the lady who came to work here for an easy life in 1985, joining *Clinton Cards* as a bought ledger clerk, a job well beneath her considerable abilities. This was probably her downfall as it was obvious that she was far too good for the job she was doing. When I found myself without a secretary for a couple of weeks I asked Alice, my office manager, to find someone to step into the breach and she instantly thought of the new lady in accounts. Valerie didn't have a clue what she was letting herself in for… neither did I probably. I remember saying to her, "Before you accept, I don't want somebody who cries easily!"

THINK OF A CARD...

For the past 23 years Valerie has been invaluable, turning her hand to whatever needs doing... and having to deal with my rather enthusiastic management style to boot. I'm probably not supposed to know it, but other staff – directors included – will ask Valerie to approach me on a particular issue if they are not sure how I might react. On the rare occasion when reinforcements are required, my brother Alan is drawn in to mediate as well! Valerie protects me from unwanted calls and performs all sorts of tasks well beyond the call of duty. I've even been known to phone her at home in the middle of the night if I am abroad and need something urgently.

As the months passed and I got used to *Clinton Cards* being a listed company, I accepted the fact that shares are only 'paper money', not being worth anything until they are sold. I am much more relaxed about minor deviations now that I have seen swings in both directions over the past 20-odd years, but I found it difficult not to take it personally, especially in the early days.

I was also acutely aware of the people with a small number of shares, perhaps 50 or 100, who had taken a risk on us, most of them our customers who believe in what we stand for. I am less worried about the City institutions and pension funds (despite the fact that they have far more influence on the share price) – they can take care of themselves. I gain much more satisfaction seeing the share price increase and knowing that the ordinary people Margaret Thatcher encouraged to buy shares have seen a modest return for their risk. Not wanting to appear too altruistic, a healthy share price doesn't do me any harm either!

However, if you play by City rules and want the benefits of being able to raise capital to grow, you have to take it on the chin when things go the wrong way. As might have become apparent, I have never been a big fan of overpaid City types who take huge commissions from profits generated by ordinary working people. If they get it wrong, their bonus might be reduced, but some poor bloke who has invested his whole life in a particular industry sees all his hard work torn to shreds.

For example, one day I saw the price drop by 22p following an item in the press speculating that we'd had a poor Christmas... and it was just that, speculation. Similarly, our shares are attacked if something happens to the retail market, like *Burtons*, *Next*, or even *Ratners* to quote a well-documented example. But our business is different and is more recession-proof than most. As I have said before, even if people are a bit strapped for cash, they still send cards to their friends and relatives... they may not send a present, but cards are rarely forsaken.

A so-called expert can speculate about our share price, yet I rarely get to meet these experts. I would love to extend the challenge to meet them and see who knows more about the greeting card industry – them or me. I know where my money lies!

Then there is that old bugbear of takeovers. If I had a pound for every time I heard that some company or other was interested in buying *Clinton Cards*, I could afford to retire. However, I tend to be philosophical about this, taking the view that while they are having a go at us they are leaving someone else alone. It may be tomorrow's fish and chip paper, but in the meantime our business suffers until the hack moves on to some other poor soul.

Occasionally I have had to make people redundant; it is part of business life and sometimes cannot be helped. However, there was one redundancy which really got to me because it was largely out of my hands. We were having a tough time in the City and we needed to make some cutbacks. The chap concerned was just in the wrong place at the wrong time, and I felt it was the least I could do to tell him myself. It was one of the hardest things I have ever had to do and I hope I never have to again. Even now, years later, I still feel awkward about this and feel pangs of discomfort.

I also know that the City does not take kindly to family companies. I can understand that there could be a tendency to promote by name rather than ability, but I am passionate about my business and have been so for 40 years, and I would not let Clinton get his hands on one shop, let alone all of them, if I did not have confidence in his ability. He has proved himself time and time again and he knows the business better than anyone I know... with perhaps one exception! And my daughter Debbie is no mug either. She, too, has learned the business the hard way, from the very bottom. Our motivating factor has always been the same, to provide customers with exceptional value and to be profitable. It's never been important for me to have a big office block with a fancy boardroom. We've always been shop floor directors, not golfing ones.

I should mention that by this time Debbie had joined the company. Unsurprisingly, she had worked as a Saturday girl in the Chingford shop whilst still at school. If I'm honest, I wondered if this might make her see the light and plead with me for a full-time job on leaving school, but I should have known my daughter better. She was adamant that she was not going to follow in her brother's footsteps, preferring a career in public relations, because 'it sounded glamorous'.

Like most people leaving school, Debbie did not know what she really wanted to do. I didn't mind that, and I like to think I would have supported her in whatever career she chose, but that was the problem – she didn't know what she wanted to do and she was making little effort in looking for a job to help pay the rent! Debbie was living the life of Riley, swanning around with her school friend who had a similar attitude towards work... or, rather, the lack of it. Well, I wasn't having it and so I gave her an ultimatum: "If you intend to live at home, you're coming into the office with me on Monday morning until you find something better to do. You need to understand why people have to get up in the morning." Being a chip off the old block, she could give as good as she got, and so came back at me with, "I'm not going to be trapped like Clinton!" My reply to this was, "I don't want to trap you... I've got enough trouble with your brother!"

The upshot was that Debbie grudgingly came into the office with me on the Monday morning and, thankfully, she didn't find anything better to do. Debbie learnt the business the hard way, starting at the lowest level and doing everything that was asked of her. All the experiences were useful, not least when it came to managing her own staff, but she really shone once she'd discovered her forte in product development... after all, what girl doesn't like shopping with her dad's money!

In true Ronnie Corbett style, I seem to have deviated from the situation back in 1989. Thankfully the half-year figures since the

USM flotation were good and the City loved us. As the *Financial Times* reported on 4th April 1989:

Clinton Cards Unveils a 63% Increase

In its first figures since coming to the USM last April, *Clinton Cards*, the specialist greeting card retailer, unveiled a 63% expansion in pre-tax profits.

The outcome, up from £1.52m to £2.51m was posted on turnover, excluding VAT, of £20.8m (13.18m). Earnings per 10p share were hoisted 44% to 12.84p and the proposed final dividend is 2.53p for a total of 3.53p.

* * *

The next milestone for me came when I heard about the availability of a shop in Bromley High Street, a most prestigious area. This was not just any old shop, but a 3,500 sq ft, three-storey affair. To put it in context, this was one-third the size of the head office we bought in Loughton in 1984, and Bromley prices are a little more than warehouses in Loughton. Indeed, it was the price of the shop which shook me, and for once I was a little indecisive.

I was used to hammering out terms for shops with Ray Cottington of *Dudley, Samuel, Harrison* who would fax over 'Goad plans' of the various high streets and shopping malls. The Goad plans detailed all the shops, the size of units and the location etc. Ray had a habit of phoning late in the afternoon and we would continue well into the evening discussing the nuances of what was right for us, and the price of course.

Ray was a great guy, a man I could relate to – after all, he was an East End lad too. We built up a very good working relationship over the years as we were on the same wavelength. Ray was not a 'yes man' and would give as good as he got, and I respected that. On several occasions I tried to persuade Ray to come out for lunch so that we could mix business with pleasure. This was quite exceptional for me as I have never been one for fancy long lunches. Ray extolled a similar work ethic and it was several years before he would concede to visiting our offices at lunchtime, but even then I could not persuade him to waste time going out to lunch. Valerie provided cheese sandwiches while Ray and I pored over the Goad plans. To make it a bit more special she tarted up the tray with a few fancy bits and pieces fitting for this special occasion. Valerie and I got to know Ray well and it was a very sad day when we attended his funeral after his untimely death in 1996 at far too young an age in his early forties.

There might have been Goad plans involved with the Bromley store, but this was where the similarities ended. The dealings were conducted through solicitors, and I remember several demanding negotiations sitting in John Coleman's office. The price on the table was a lot of money and I needed to think about it. It would certainly help raise our profile having such a prestigious flagship store, and there was no denying the number of potential customers who were likely to pass through the shop… but we were talking about a lot of money, despite this being a time of lower than usual rents due to a downturn in the retail sector. All this money was before we even added overheads like shop fittings, utilities and paying for the considerable number of staff required to run the shop. We would have to sell an awful lot of cards to break even, let alone make any sort of profit.

Rose was with me when I popped into John's office to give him my final decision. I had just about convinced myself to go ahead with it, but John, forever the conservative legal man, gave the counter argument and persuaded me not to proceed. Rose was very surprised because she was not used to seeing me as anything other than gung-ho as far as selling cards was concerned. After all, wasn't I the one who kept telling her that cards are recession-proof and that people will always buy them? That we Brits are a sentimental lot who appreciate our friends and family and like to tell them so?

It was a strange feeling turning down this opportunity to announce to the world that *Clinton Cards* – with such a high-profile, three-storey shop – had arrived. As I reached the door of John's office on my way out, I couldn't live with my decision. Where was that unshakeable belief in everything I had worked for over the past 20 years? I had no choice. I turned round and instructed him to proceed. Once the decision had been made, calm returned.

John and I have since joked about this many times and he is the first to admit that it would have been wrong not to proceed with the Bromley store, not least because it was a stepping stone to bigger and better things. John has often advised caution, and I suppose that is part of a solicitor's job – after all, he was only trying to protect me. But since when has caution ever been part of an entrepreneur's armoury? Don't get me wrong; it is important not to be cavalier, and I never want to be, not least because it's my money I'm dealing with.

But *Clinton Cards* would never have become the success story it is today if I had always erred on the side of caution. Risks have to be taken in business, hopefully calculated risks, but risks nonetheless. And as with all risks the rewards can be great... or they can end in disaster.

This decision to proceed with the store in Bromley High Street was an important milestone. It had helped me to think big, and there was nothing bigger than another opportunity which soon came my way... a shop in Oxford Street, one of the greatest shopping experiences on the planet. Being similar in size to the Bromley High Street shop, again on three storeys, this really would be the ultimate flagship store. The decision was not just an ego trip. The figures stacked up and a couple of months later I was pleased to read that financial analysts applauded my decision.

Clinton Cards
The USM Magazine – May 1989

The Essex based greeting card retailer is proving the exception to tales of woe emanating from the specialist retail sector at present. It was very dependent on Christmas trade, with 94% of profits coming through in the second half to the end of January, but it has shown that the current squeeze on spending in the high interest rate climate is not affecting it at all. In fact, quite the opposite could be true, in that if the squeeze deepens, then a birthday or a Christmas card would probably not be sacrificed although a present or gift could be. But more than that, *Clinton* is, we believe, capitalising very successfully indeed on the specialist greeting card concept and the changing needs of the UK consumer in this area.

We in the UK are already the largest spender, per head, on greeting cards than anywhere else in the world, including the incredibly card conscious US, and we are buying those cards in increasing numbers from specialist retailers. *Clinton* has around 12% of the card market bought from specialists, but only 3% of the overall market, and with the trend swinging its way it is extremely well placed to take full advantage from its existing shops alone. Of course the company is also expanding its outlets at a significant rate, and opened 43 new shops during the year, taking numbers up from 77 to the current 114, a 60% increase. The average number of shops open during the last reporting period was around 90, which produced turnover of £20m excluding VAT, and pre-tax profits of £2.5m, up from £1.5m last time.

During the year it also made three small acquisitions, but stripping out both these and the new sites opened from scratch, the organic growth of the existing outlets, year on year, was a very impressive 15%, approximately twice the rate of inflation.

Since the year end the group has opened a massive, for them, 3,500 sq ft flagship store in central London, in Oxford Street, very close to *John Lewis*. The move heralds the start of the long awaited drive into Central London where, aside from a small outlet near Liverpool Street Station in the City (apparently very strong on 'Sorry to see you leaving your job' cards!) the group has not been represented up until now. It has traditionally concentrated its efforts south and east of a line between the Wash and, say, Portsmouth, and even though it is well represented here, it still sees scope for an additional 200 shops in this area alone, without the need to spread further afield.

At present some quite small towns support two and sometimes even three *Clinton Cards* shops, often in the same high street, which is as good an indication as any of the underlying demand for the group's greeting cards and other items, which include *Garfield* and other character merchandise (mostly soft toys), gift wrappings, ribbon and paper.

Acquisitions may well play a role in the group's development in the future, and with £2m in cash at the year end (since depleted by the near £1m opening of the flagship store above) the group is well placed to take advantage of opportunities as they present themselves.

Even without this, organic growth is strong enough for us to forecast a significant profit increase this year, even in this slightly difficult retail climate, and we would expect pre-tax profits of around £3.2m for the year to end January 1990, for earnings per share of 15.4p and a prospective P/E of 12 with the shares at the current 195p.

Much depends on the Christmas 1989 trade, of course, with well over 90% of profits earned in the second half, but such is the momentum within the group that we think that this forecast will turn out to be conservative. At this level the shares look excellent value to us and should be bought; this is a specialist retailer that is indeed helping to change the shopping habits of a nation and its success in this respect has so far gone largely unnoticed.

* * *

Praise indeed... how long would it last!

I am pleased to report that their estimates of £3.2m pre-tax profits were exceeded... we made £3.44m that year, a 37% rise.

Despite having a go at the City boys, some analysts do know their stuff and provide great detail for investors. The *Barclays de Zoete Wedd* study was one such, writing the following about our Oxford Street store. Read it carefully, because I'll be asking questions later!

Barclays de Zoete Wedd
March 1990

Of the new stores acquired to the year end January 1990, the most significant was that of their flagship store in Oxford Street which was acquired in April 1989 for a £1m premium. With over 3,000 sq ft, the Oxford Street store is almost double the average of

1,750 sq ft per store. The location of the Oxford Street store and the high customer flow suggest that this store should yield significant returns. This prompts two questions: how much are the returns likely to be and will these justify the premium paid for them?

Estimating the *average* figure for the pre-tax profit/sq ft evens out these differentials between stores. Location is a fundamental determinant of PBT (profit before tax)/sq ft. With this in mind, the PBT/sq ft figure for the Oxford Street site is likely to be significantly higher than most other locations.

Using the 1990 figures, the pre-tax profits/sq ft will be £14. For an average shop with about 1,800 sq ft this would imply a PBT of £25,000. With a base of fixed assets per average shop of £93,000, the ratio PBT to the fixed asset base is 0.27.

Are you following?

If we translate to the Oxford Street shop of 3,000 sq ft, the equivalent figures are a PBT of £42,000, created from a base of £155,000 fixed assets. If we then add in the premium paid for the Oxford Street site to its base of fixed assets, this implies that this shop should yield PBT of well over £312,000 to achieve the PBT/fixed asset ratio. The Oxford Street shop is anticipated to earn a PBT of £42,000, but the sum of its fixed assets suggest that it should yield £312,000, which is over seven times expected earnings.

This calculation gives a very rough idea of the sort of returns the Oxford Street site should yield to be able to justify the premium paid for it. It is likely that the Oxford Street shop will yield significantly more than the other sites because of its location. So far, Don Lewin is very pleased with this shop's performance believing it to be equivalent to 11 or 12 units.

* * *

Boy oh boy! If I had any idea of all this when I answered that ad in the paper from Abba Rivlin and Maurice Fern, I may have had second thoughts! Seriously, though, such analysis is important and it is the sort of thing our number-crunchers are looking at all the time... although they do present it to me in a slightly more digestible format.

One of the best articles I read on our business at this time was also from a financial institution, *County NatWest*, but it had a much more down-to-earth style, appropriate for the more modest investor of the type Mrs T was encouraging. I include it here as it provides a succinct yet insightful view into our work, reflecting my philosophy better than I could express it myself.

County NatWest
Summer 1989

Every year, the UK population buys cards at roughly the rate of 36 each. Even though they buy nearly half of them at Christmas, that still leaves a lot of business to be done during the remainder of the year. It is this business which the specialist seeks to attract. *Clinton Cards* is one of a new breed of aggressive card retailers aiming to dominate the market.

Many retailers look on cards as a once a year, seasonal item, useful for a little bit of extra turnover at Christmas. During the remainder of the year they put the space to what they consider to be more productive use.

Specialists look at the problem differently. They see over one million birthdays a week; each of which will result in cards from at least the immediate family and often from friends as well. Beyond that there are other established occasions like Valentine's Day, Easter, and Mother's and Father's Day. There are also other personal events eg wedding anniversaries, 'get well', 'congratulations' and 'engagements'.

Britons already send more cards than any other nation so there is little organic growth in the volume of cards sent. It can probably be quantified at 12% each year, which fits comfortably with population growth among the prime card buyers. It is in value terms that growth is moving faster – up about 10% each year as the market demands more and more sophistication. The essence of the *Clinton* offer has always been an extensive selection of the best cards at reasonably high prices from the best space in any high street.

Don Lewin, the founder and chairman of *Clinton Cards* was one of the first to realise that cards could be sold from prime high street space and that customers would pay a premium for choice.

When the company was founded in 1968, most cards were sold through CTNs [Confectionery/ tobacconist/newsagent outlets], but he was confident that better presentation and more exclusivity would attract more customers.

Throughout the 1970s the company grew relatively slowly (it was effectively sold and re-started in 1972) as the offer was refined and developed. It is really only in the last five years that consumer affluence has reached a level that has allowed rapid development of specialist outlets. Don Lewin and his team, which includes his son after whom the chain is named, were ready to take advantage of the propitious conditions.

With the very rapid rate of expansion, attracting staff and particularly managers could have been a bit of a problem. But, as one of the few growth companies in retailing, *Clinton Cards* can obviously attract some of the more ambitious people available.

Besides that, it has its own staff training programme to develop a steady stream of managers to open shops. At an opening they are always helped by an experienced relief manager and the area manager. The remainder of the staff are mostly part-timers but all are trained by the manager to increase their knowledge of the product range and encourage repeat purchases.

The formula has been proven over the buoyant spending years of the 1980s, but the company has undertaken precipitate expansion in the face of what promises to be a spending slowdown in the South East. There is little doubt, however, that *Clinton* will eventually emerge as a leading player in the upper reaches of the card market, but hopes of a smooth path, while squeezed between rising costs and declining retail sales, are somewhat optimistic.

* * *

We had experienced an amazing few years, and since flotation *Clinton Cards* shares had risen £1 to 250p. With everything on the up and up, in May 1990 I decided that we should celebrate with a £6.4m rights issue and a move up to the Official Stock Exchange List.

That went well, with a 97% acceptance, and by the end of the year we had over 200 shops and a share price approaching £3. This City lark was easy! A more significant milestone on the world stage was the departure of Margaret Thatcher as Prime Minister in November 1990. Her premiership was one in which *Clinton Cards* had flourished. It made me wonder how a less strong leader might fare, and what the implications would be for the business world in general and *Clinton Cards* in particular. Only time would tell.

8 | A Decade of Milestones

So far so good – everything in the garden looked rosy and despite the recession we continued to do well. This was reflected in our bullish 1990 Company Report.

> We estimate that we are now the largest specialist greeting card retailer in the country, but that we still only have a 4.5% share of the total market. The growth of the greeting card market is being generated by specialist card shops who have increased their market share from 22% to 27% in the last two years. *Clinton Cards* has been very much at the forefront of this expansion and we believe that there is enormous scope for us to continue developing our position as the country's pre-eminent specialist greeting card retailer.

Our next step was to venture north of the Watford Gap when we acquired the twelve shops of the *Selectacard* group, mainly based around Manchester and Liverpool.

As the economy was beginning to feel the pinch, greeting cards were the place to be, something advocated by *The Independent* newspaper on Monday 24th December 1990.

A greeting card says more about you than plastic money ever can. It is the least expensive option to fulfil your seasonal obligations without attracting the bailiffs.

If, like me, you have long passed your credit limit, the only remedy is to buy loved ones – and those you can't afford to ignore – a nice Christmas card. And you avoid Christmas crowds to hunt for presents which the recipients probably would not touch with a bargepole.

For most people the purchase of cards – for birthdays, illness, Mother's Day or for the Valentine next-door – is an increasingly popular habit.

Not surprisingly *Clinton Cards*, the specialist card retailer, is doing a roaring trade. While many high street retailers are feeling the pinch, *Clinton* is continuing to enjoy a healthy demand. "Trading has been pretty good and I have been pleasantly surprised by the strength of demand despite the gloom and doom," says Don Lewin, *Clinton's* chairman and chief executive.

He says the sales patterns this season have been the same as in previous years. Humorous cards, as always, have been popular.

* * *

Such optimism was reflected in the results, this time quoted from the *Evening Standard*.

Cards Deliver for Clinton

Christmas cards come cheaper than presents, so perhaps it wasn't too surprising that in the recession-hit year to last January, *Clinton Cards* romped home with a 46% rise in profits to record £5.02 million.

Earnings per share rose 22% to 20.4p and *Clinton* is pushing up its full-year dividend 24% to 5.25p. It expanded into 62 new shops during the year and traded from 225 at the year-end.

* * *

However, from here on 1991 was not a year I'd like to repeat as, despite a successful rights issue, our share price fell significantly. We had sailed through the post Black Monday recession in the late 1980s almost unscathed, but this recession was different. We weren't seeing the same number of people on the high street. I have always been confident that people will buy cards whatever happens to the economy – after all, our products reflect a relatively small part of the family budget. They might cut down on clothes, homeware and eating out, but people are always prepared to spend a couple of quid on a friend. This was different, though; people weren't even going shopping. We rely on passing trade, and if people are not out passing our shops they certainly aren't going to be able to buy.

However, I believe that you find real character when backs are against the wall. Everyone finds it easy when things are on the up and up – it is only in adversity that you can see a person's true worth, and my answer to the adversity was to expand. I knew the business better than anyone, and what we had been doing well for the past 20-plus years hadn't suddenly turned bad overnight. It is often the same with football. A player has a couple of bad games and starts getting written off, but he doesn't become a bad player overnight. We stood for quality, and even if the City was happy to forecast doom and gloom I was determined to stand up for what I knew to be true, so I put my money where my mouth was and went on an expansion drive.

It is fortunate that most of our customers are only interested in buying cards – and good ones at that. Whether our share price is 500p or 50p does not mean a jot to them, as long as they can find the card they want in our shops.

If you believed the City scare mongering, I would have been investing in a large supply of tablets for my impending overdose. Nothing was further from my mind, not least because during a recession there are bargains to be had, and for us this meant reduced rents. In my book, reduced rents means more shops. Our costs might have risen with expansion, but I have always been very careful when it comes to cashflow, and over-stretching ourselves is not a policy I would ever adopt.

Being quoted on the stock exchange also brings other pressures, not least talk about possible takeovers. The supposed predator in this instance was *WH Smith*, followed soon after by *John Menzies*, and I had to fend off countless calls from financial journalists trying to add two and two. All I can say is that for financial journalists they were rotten at arithmetic judging by some of the stories I read.

The Times
26 January 1992

WH SMITH, the retailing group that includes *Our Price* record shops and *Waterstones*, the bookseller, is considering a takeover offer for *Clinton Cards*, the 236-strong chain of greeting card shops.

WH Smith is keen to set up a specialist greetings card chain and has recently opened two trial shops in Cheltenham and Ilford. *Clinton*, a family firm founded in 1968, is the largest card chain in the country.

WH Smith's board has recently discussed an offer for *Clinton*, according to a source close to the company. The board considered the price it would have to pay for control and decided it was an attractive deal, said the source.

Any deal with *Clinton* would have to be agreed because Don Lewin, the chairman, and his son, Clinton, managing director, control more than 50% of the shares.

Analysts believe that, long term, *Clinton* could do well. Borrowings are low and the company will benefit quickly from an upturn in consumer spending.

Still, there was one good thing to come from all this takeover talk – it pushed up our share price as all the speculators sought to make a killing. For once I was quite happy to stand by and read such piffle in the press!

Whilst it is prudent to keep an eye on the competition, I have preferred to back my own instincts and concentrate on what I can control, and for me that is *Clinton Cards*. We had expansion plans of our own – plans that proved to be sound as we doubled the number of shops over the next five years.

There was also other negative publicity in the press in 1991. This concerned our initiative to introduce a new range of cards... divorce cards. Apparently these did not go down well with certain sections of the clergy. Fortunately, we didn't see the clergy as a big market for divorce cards... but most other people took them with the humour we intended and they sold like hot cakes. One card read:

Thinking of You on Your Divorce

So the match of the day is over...
time to start thinking about a transfer
before you get relegated.
Good luck for the future.

I have always believed the greeting card industry to be robust, and so it proved with the recession of the early 1990s. Our headaches were short-lived compared with other sectors of the market. We were one of the last to be hit by the recession and one of the first out, and I was satisfied that we were able to turn a loss of £163,000 into a profit of £2.3 million in one year.

Whilst not a particularly enjoyable time to endure, I felt that we gained as a company in other ways. I have always been paranoid about wasting money, and I hate it when others take it upon themselves to do so on my behalf. Some people seem to think that companies operate under a different system and that anything from fiddling expenses to pilfering office stationery is fair game. I can state categorically that no one in my company is under that misapprehension, or at least if they are and they are discovered, their days are numbered.

Those who had joined *Clinton Cards* after the flotation and had only seen a rise in the share price began to realise that shares can go down as well as up... as all financial advisers now have to remind investors. The occasional reminder to staff does not go amiss either, and I am sure that the experience of the recession was not wasted.

In 1992 we introduced a range of cards for the blind and visually impaired. It came to my attention that cards were not available for this section of society and so we arranged for a trial of Braille cards. Over 20,000 cards were sold over the 1991 Christmas period in a limited number of shops, so we made the decision to make them available universally. This time the decision was met with a better press I'm pleased to report.

A feature less welcomed, as far as I was concerned, was Sunday trading. I am not looking at this from a religious point of view, although I can appreciate the argument that keeping one day special for the family has its merits. If people want to shop that's fine, but from the stance of the retailer and the shop worker other factors have to be taken into consideration. I said at the time, and the facts have now confirmed this, that once Sunday trading was introduced it would be the thin end of the wedge.

It makes sense for DIY stores and garden centres to open on a Sunday, as this is a time when they are in great demand. The same does not hold for all shops, but once the floodgates have been opened they cannot be shut. If the majority of shops in a high street or shopping mall are open we are virtually forced into doing the same unless we are to lose trade, and, as I've said before, once customers find another outlet they may start using it more frequently.

For many retailers late night opening and Sunday trading means just one thing: increased costs. Shops that were once open between 9.00 am and 5.00 pm for five-and-a-half days a week (remember half-day closing?) are now open for seven days, and two or three of those might be until 9.00 pm. What was once 44 hours a week is now more like 68 hours, an increase of 54%. Additionally, many of these extra hours incur higher wage rates, increasing costs further. Income does not increase proportionately in many retail establishments – far from it – so from a purely financial point of view it doesn't make sense.

I really hope the situation does not worsen and become like shopping areas in the United States which are like ghost towns during the day as people can spread their shopping until very late at night, every night of the week. I believe that, ultimately, longer shopping hours will damage retailing in the UK.

To dip our toe in the water of technology, in 1993 we introduced 'Creatacard', enabling customers to completely design and

Think of a card!

Opening our 500th shop - Cribbs Causeway, Bristol, 1998

The opening of the world's largest greeting card shop, Oxford Street, 1999

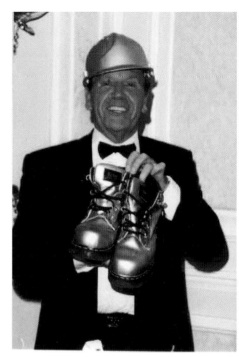

Rob Winfield presenting me with new boots and helmet after mine had been nicked during the development of our flagship Oxford Street store

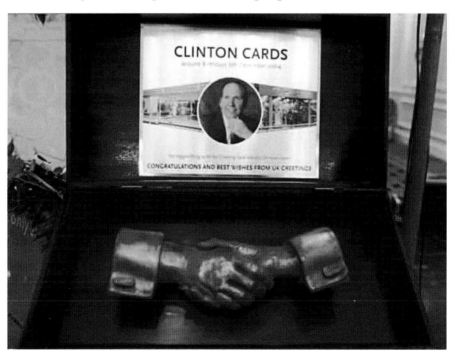

Some of our wonderful service personnel
receiving their Christmas cards

Guide Dog for the Blind, Clinton

Opening the Business and Enterprise Centre at West Hatch High School

With Bert Weedon presenting a minibus to Kingsdown School

Clinton and Julie

Debbie and George

Outside the Palace with my family

Comparing awards - sharing a joke with my old friend,
Don Coombe MBE

I've always been a bit of a crooner, but a highlight was to share the stage with Jimmy Tarbuck and Kenny Lynch

Debbie running the London Marathon

Messing about on the river

It's been a privilege for Rose and me to meet some great people

With the great Lady, Mrs T

Board of Directors

Brian Jackson (non-exec), Robert Gunlack (non-exec), John Coleman (non-exec),
John Robinson, Mike Bugler, Stuart Houlston,
Debbie Darlington, Barry Hartog, Don Lewin, Clinton Lewin

Alan and Jean, Don and Rose, Don and Betty, Ron and Tel, Brian and Valerie

I know my place!

Party time!

Thank you, Rose

It's been fun

personalise their own greeting cards, which they watch being drawn in colour whilst they wait.

To celebrate our 25th birthday we acquired a further 19 shops from *Carlton Cards*, having bought ten the previous autumn. This brought our total number of shops to 275, so why not have a celebration! However, I was taken aback by the 'sea of suits' in my office on the morning of the anniversary party, my immediate reaction being that we must have a problem. The only problem was opening the champagne... but I was happy to cope with that!

I have always been ribbed in the family about what cards they can buy for me. As they say, "What card do you buy the man who sells millions of them?" However, they got their own back in style when it came to Father's Day in 1993, having commissioned a card measuring 5ft by 2ft 6ins. For good measure, Debbie being in charge of marketing, they had 500 printed so that at least one was available in each of our shops, bearing the claim, 'The World's Largest Father's Day Card'. Selling them was not a problem... although I'm not sure how the Royal Mail coped with deliveries!

I was also on the receiving end of another in-joke when Valerie made a big show of presenting me with a card on Boss's Day... after all it was me who introduced the concept into Britain! I was also relieved that I had remembered to send her a card on Secretary's Day... and that she had not had to remind me about it as she usually does with most of my other cards!

The boy band, 'Take That', may have tens of thousands of girls swooning at their feet, and millions of fans throughout the world, but as far as *Clinton Cards* is concerned, they were no match for Mr Blobby. Christmas 1993 saw 70,000 Mr Blobbies leap off the shelves. Take That the following year made little impact on Mr Blobby's impressive figure. We had to wait another couple of years before we saw the likes of it again. Indeed, Wallace and Gromit outstripped even Mr Blobby as the larger branches were selling out within an hour of new stock arriving.

My son Clinton had been a slave to work for many years, so much so that he even decided to marry someone in the industry. He knew he had arrived when the event made the City Diary section of the *Daily Telegraph* for 23rd August 1994.

Well-Versed in Nuptials Stake

There was no shortage of cards at the Essex wedding last Saturday, of Clinton Lewin to Julie Butterfield. Lewin is managing director of *Clinton Cards*, which was named after him by his father, the founder chairman, Don Lewin.

The couple met through business when the new Mrs Lewin worked for *Carlton Cards*, one of *Clinton's* suppliers.

Excessive references to cards in the speeches was predictable I suppose, but even the vicar banged on about them. Clinton took the opportunity to point out that sales of wedding cards are up 20% this year. The chief bridesmaid, incidentally, was Debbie Lewin, Clinton's sister and marketing director.

* * *

Two months after Clinton tied the knot, we had our own union, with *Hallmark*, one of our major suppliers, bringing to fruition many months of negotiations and many years of personal ambition. I had always admired what *Hallmark* stood for and the quality of their cards. Additionally, their 86 shops in England and Wales were a good fit with only twelve overlapping sites, bringing our tally up to 360 shops.

In the UK most of *Hallmark's* shops traded under the name The Hall of Cards, but various other names included Smart Idea, Mary Morrison, Tru' Love, Just for You, Vickerstaffs, Cresta Cards, Occasions, Ace of Cards and Expressions. Many of these had been acquired by *Hallmark* over the years, but when *Hallmark UK* merged its operation with *The Andrew Brownsword Collection*, it was decided that owning and running retail outlets was not part of the company's core business and consequently they were happy to sell the shops to us.

This was seen as an eminently sensible move – it must have been because the *FT* said so:

> *Clinton Cards'* acquisition of the *Hallmark* shops seems to make sense for the card retailer. The stores should need little work to fixtures and fittings and will be trading for *Clinton* over the busy Christmas period.
>
> Moreover, *Clinton's* repayments are attractively linked to its demand for *Hallmark* goods over the next four years. The interim results are worse than last year, but not as gloomy as expected after this summer's profits warning. The group is thought to

have improved cost control and should be in a good position to benefit when consumer confidence returns. Analysts forecast pre-tax profits of about £2m for the year, which gives a prospective multiple of 13.7 on yesterday's close of 103p, up 2p. For those confident of an upturn in consumer spending, the shares have scope for further recovery.

* * *

This transaction was also significant to me in achieving another personal milestone. When I answered that advert placed by Abba Rivlin and Maurice Fern all those years before, *WH Smith* was far and away the biggest retailer of greeting cards. If you'd have told me then that one day my company would surpass them as market leader, I would have thought you were mad, but that is precisely what had just happened. As *Hall of Cards* accounted for 1½% of the market, this brought our share to 9%, one per cent greater than *WH Smith*. *The Sun* newspaper even christened me the 'King of Cards'... what more could I hope for!

Being competitive by nature, I have always found that targets help to focus the mind. I'm pleased to see that the government has finally got wise to this, reversing its trend of non-competitive sports in schools. It might have taken the prospect of the Olympics on home soil to have instigated this, but at least it did.

With *Clinton Cards* now market leader in the high street for selling greeting cards I needed a new target and I set my sights on 1,000 shops. I was confident that there was room in the market for this, as we were still largely based in the south of England at this time. It is not that I am driven by numbers for the sake of numbers, but I feel that a target helps motivate me and the whole team. We were doing something right, and I felt it my duty to continue to strive for greater excellence, not just for new customers but for our current customers. You can always get better, and the day I feel I have achieved everything I can is the day I'll retire.

One thousand shops seemed a long way off, but in September 1995 it came a step closer when we bought 112 shops from the US supplier *Carlton Cards*. Not only did this bring our tally to 484 shops, it gave us a presence in dozens of new areas of the country as well as Scotland for the first time.

There were many articles in the press at this time, but the one I include appeared in *Greetings*, the magazine of the greeting card industry, as this provides a more detailed account of where we were at the time.

The Man Behind the News... Don Lewin

Picking up a plush Sumo wrestler, epitomising his characteristic instinctive choices, which market tested well on Father's Day and will no doubt be a major money-spinner for Valentine's Day, Don Lewin explains his success as an ability to sell and gut instinct.

It is this gut instinct and hard graft that has taken him from a salesman to running the largest UK chain with 484 retail outlets. He started his retail career by borrowing £1,000 to open one shop in Epping, in 1968. *Clinton Cards*, whose motto 'only the best is good enough' is now, Don claims, the largest specialist card chain in the world and accounts for 11% of the entire UK greeting card market worth £1bn.

The company employs around 3,500 people in the UK and when on a recent visit to a plush factory in Java one third of the staff of 2,000 was devoted to *Clinton* products. Don said this gave him a real 'buzz'.

The recent acquisition of 112 *Carlton* card shops gives *Clinton* comprehensive representation across the UK. Don emphasised that despite the size of the operation – the company has just acquired new premises of 20,000 sq ft nearby to cope with the newly extended departments – this is still a family firm. Son Clinton, 33 is managing director and daughter Debbie, 27, is marketing director.

He is himself an unassuming affable character, and although on friendly terms with John Major, whom he'd replace with Maggie Thatcher any day, he maintains a direct and honest approach with all he meets.

A true patriot and lifelong Tory, the company lobby is adorned with paintings of the Queen, Winston Churchill and Maggie Thatcher. You certainly know where you stand with this man. One of his major suppliers described him as "firm but fair." An ideal maxim for a father and a company director.

He is proud to say he has done every job in the business – this gives him credibility with his employees, as he really does understand what is expected and it means that you can't pull the wool over his eyes.

It is quite clear to him at the outset that in order to make his mark on the industry the product would have to be very high quality to stand out from what was on offer, and this applies today. He went on to explain why he was one of the first to tie up with *Hallmark* in 1968. Don says, "I liked the *Hallmark* product because it was expensive." When asked whether this helped in *Clinton's* acquisition of *Hallmark's Hall of Cards* chain he said, "No, we were just their biggest outlet, as we are for all our suppliers. The only way anyone gets into *Clinton Cards* is by being an upmarket product. We guide our publishers and suppliers so a significant amount of product is tailor-made for us."

Publishers who supply *Clinton Cards* and other shops will supply different lines so that there is no overlap. Selection is based on the spread of card turns and it is up to the supplier to make sure he is supplying *Clinton Cards* with fast sellers.

He sums up his success as having the courage and the ability to maximise sales opportunities, a philosophy that he has practised from the earliest days when he would be selling Christmas cards on Christmas Eve when most people had run out two weeks ago.

"Running a business is common sense, and abiding by the motto that 'only the best is good enough' has served us well." Don Lewin has made an unrivalled contribution to the card industry, which others will observe closely and no doubt seek to emulate.

The article mentions my patriotism, of which I am very proud. I know it's my job to be on the lookout for sales opportunities, but I can say with hand on heart that I am firmly behind the idea of celebrating St George's Day, whether or not I sell a single card. Indeed, I belong to The Royal Society of St George, the patron of which is Her Majesty The Queen, and Vice-Presidents include the Duke of Wellington, the Duke of Westminster and Baroness Margaret Thatcher.

Imagine then my delight at receiving the following letter:

28th April 1996

Dear Sir,

May I take this opportunity of thanking you most sincerely for making St George's Day cards available this year. My sister in America was thrilled to receive hers. My mother who is in her eighties was delighted to receive a St George card for the first time in her life. She lives in sheltered accommodation and the other residents were most intrigued by the card, having never seen one before.

I hope your sales went well and that 'St George' becomes a regular in your excellent outlets.

Yours patriotically

Mrs J E

The next major milestone came with the accounts for the year ending 28th January 1996 as we had achieved an annual turnover of £100 million... not bad for a lad who left school at 15 without any qualifications! However, an even greater landmark was just around the corner...

A letter arrived from the Central Chancery of the Order of Knighthood at St James's Palace advising that I was being considered for an Order of the British Empire honour and, should a recommendation be forthcoming, would I be willing to accept? Would I be willing to accept! As everyone knows, I am an ardent royalist and patriotic to the core. I am mightily proud of Britain and our traditions and if I was considered suitable to be honoured in this way who was I to refuse?

My acceptance having been duly sent, a second letter arrived from the Central Chancery confirming the offer of the honour. Of course, everything had to be kept hush-hush, but when the honours list was announced all the excitement began again and I received dozens of cards from well-wishers as well as calls from journalists and reporters.

As I was allowed to invite three guests, I was delighted that Rose, Clinton and Debbie could accompany me for my big day at the Palace. The investiture was to be conducted by Her Majesty The Queen, and it was one of the proudest moments of my life when my name was called and I stepped forward. Usually The Queen congratulates the recipient and says a few words, but she had quite a conversation with me. As Christmas was approaching she said that I must be particularly busy, and so we were able to have a little chat. I had had the honour of meeting The Queen on previous occasions, but never to speak to like this. As I say, it was a proud and humbling experience.

With the formalities over it was time to celebrate. Arrangements had been made for a party at the *Ritz*, and what a party it was. Tel, Alan and other members of the family were there, along with many close friends, to help me celebrate this day of all days. It was great to be surrounded by the people most special to me. I have a video of the investiture which I watch from time to time. It still brings a tear to my eye.

* * *

By the autumn the share price was back beyond the 150p mark, so things were definitely on the up. In fact within the next six months it was on the better side of 250p after all our consolidations of the various acquisitions... and thanks to dear old Wallace and Gromit. Perhaps the time was ripe for more buying!

Throughout 1997 and 1998 we were hovering at just under 500 shops. It had been two-and-a-half years since we had bought the *Carlton* card shops, but it had taken time to integrate these and the *Hallmark* stores, and whilst we had also opened other shops in the meantime we just didn't seem to be able to reach that magic figure of 500.

That came when we opened the prestigious Cribbs Causeway shop in Bristol on 8th April 1998, coinciding nicely with our 30th anniversary. To mark the pearl anniversary we had a big party for employees and suppliers in the *Prince Regent Hotel*, Woodford

Bridge. It was a wonderful occasion, but even then I was waiting for the day when there would be 1,000 *Clinton Cards* shops.

But such dreams were for the future. For the time being it was a case of looking back at what had been achieved in 30 years and enjoying the party. My OBE had made it an extra-special year, and on top of that I was voted Greeting Card Personality of the Year at 'The Henries', the annual Greeting Card Awards... could a man want for more!

On
St. George's
Day

Petal by petal

A *bud* becomes a *rose* …

Year by *year*

England's

greatness grows.

9 | Sweet Charity

Before I continue with the rest of my story, now might be as good a place as any to say something about another side of the business, a side which I find very rewarding as it allows me to contribute a little and indulge some of my passions.

The final months of 1990 saw growing tensions in the Middle East as Saddam Hussein's Iraq invaded Kuwait. Events erupted the following January with the onslaught of Desert Storm. I don't like to get involved in politics, but I do feel for the individuals who get caught up in such conflicts. I may have only been in uniform for two years during my National Service, but I am fiercely proud of anyone who fights for Queen and Country and I wanted to do something to let those brave men and women know they are appreciated and not forgotten.

It struck me that I could help in a small way by supplying cards for service personnel to send back to their nearest and dearest, and in particular their mums. Mother's Day was approaching and I doubted whether such cards would be available out in the Middle East. I made some enquiries and, sure enough, I found this to be the case. Of course, this was a subject close to my heart because my own dear mum had died when I was away doing my National Service and this was a way that I could pay tribute to her memory.

THINK OF A CARD...

I thought that nothing could be easier for me than to send out a few thousand Mother's Day cards. The reality proved to be far more complicated, because reams of red tape had to be cut through before our first consignment could be shipped. I now have a far greater understanding of the logistics involved in making such a simple gesture, but where there's a will there's a way and eventually our efforts paid off.

It was gratifying to receive some very nice letters from the top and middle brass, as well as MPs, but what surprised me was the number of letters I received from privates, corporals, signalmen, chefs and the like. After all, the idea was for these people to write to their mums, not to me!

As this initiative had proved so successful, how could I not now send cards for Father's Day as well? And as Christmas approached, it was only natural that packs of Christmas cards also be sent. Since then things have snowballed and cards have been sent to many theatres of war where our troops are serving. In the region of 17,500 cards were sent in 2007.

I have had heart-warming letters from places I never knew existed, let alone how to spell, and I try to ensure I reply to every one personally. I have also had letters of appreciation from relatives back in England who have been the recipients of these cards, and, again, I aim to send each one a reply.

Over the years I have received a substantial number of letters and I keep them to re-read from time to time. I include just a few here. Obviously, names have been withheld for purposes of confidentiality, but hopefully they provide an indication of how appreciative and sensitive our service personnel are. You will see that in one letter I also received a history lesson about Mothering Sunday for good measure!

> To Mr Chairman,
>
> I just thought that I would take this opportunity to thank you very much for the box of cards. I found it very touching that somebody out there cares about us in Bosnia. I am a chef and had a really hard day's work and morale was pretty low, but I got these cards and it was a pick-me-up.
>
> Anyway, must not bore you any longer.
>
> Thank you very much
>
> Pte D M
>
> PS All the best to you and your family.

* * *

> Dear Sir,
>
> Many thanks for your contributions to 'us all' over here. It's a real morale boost for all of us here to realise there are people back home that do continue to support us in our work over here, especially over Christmas time when naturally most of the guys' morale is at its lowest.
>
> I'm a Territorial Army soldier that's currently based in Basra. When 'the war' first started I

wasn't particularly in favour of it, however, I was determined to support our boys and regularly sent welfare parcels and letters to friends of mine from my T.A. Unit that had been mobilised for the initial conflict. As the time went on and I saw the job that was left for the coalition forces to do, and thought that no matter how small I could make a contribution to the clear-up, stabilisation and rebuilding of Iraq, myself and few friends volunteered and have come out for a 6-month tour attached to the regular Army Units based out here.

It is absolutely amazing the speed and progress of the rebuilding process, and the friendly nature of the locals is really a boost after some of the negative images as seen on TV.

So, once again, thanks for supporting us – it does make a difference to us! And please continue to do so.

R A (L/Cpl)

* * *

Dear Sir/Madam,

I am writing to you on behalf of all the British Forces personnel to wish you a Happy New Year and to say thanx for the Christmas cards you generously donated to us over the festive season.

Your kind generosity was very much appreciated, not only by the troops who were unable to get hold of cards, but by our friends and families who enjoyed receiving Christmas wishes from their loved ones out here in Iraq.

I will not be surprised if my grandmother writes to you, as she was overwhelmed with the Christmas wish that she had received from me. This is all down to your kind thoughts to all the Forces.

Unfortunately we didn't get a white Christmas, but thanx to you and others we had a very merry Christmas.

Thank you once again, and I hope you have a great New Year.

Yours faithfully,

P G (Sig)

* * *

Dear Mr Lewin,

I would like to express my thanks to you for enabling my son to send me a Mother's Day card.

On this Mother's Day, as on many others in the past, he was a long way from home serving Queen and country. This year I was very surprised and pleased to receive a card from Afghanistan, which had been provided by you and your company. He and his colleagues had tried, without success, to buy cards from the PX shop, so were pleased to have your cards provided for them. I am sure many more mums were also thrilled to receive a card.

Thanks once again.

Yours sincerely

Mrs L M

* * *

Dear Mr Lewin,

Our son is serving with the Army in Afghanistan and has been since the beginning of December and hopes to be home by the end of June, having also fought in the war with Iraq.

It was with absolute delight that I received a Mothering Sunday card from him – he says that somehow he managed to get one out there – and having just taken it down from the mantelpiece, I happened to look at the back – and there was the Union Flag and notification of how it got to Afghanistan.

I am therefore writing to thank you for your thoughtfulness in sending cards out to our troops, no matter where they are, and to let you know how much this meant to me, his mother. He is facing all sorts of worries and dangers out there. He is in command of troops on the Uzbekistan border, so he has quite an onerous task. Thank you from the bottom of my heart.

May I, with the greatest delicacy in the world, just add that the day is actually called 'Mothering Sunday' and not the Americanised 'Mother's Day'! It originates from Victorian times when girls in service were allowed home, just once a year, to visit their mothers and take them a present provided by their employer. It always falls on the fourth Sunday in Lent and is remembered by special church services. It is becoming increasingly difficult these days to find cards with Mothering Sunday on them – the majority have Mother's Day. I mention this as maybe *Clinton Cards* could be persuaded to print a percentage of their cards with the beloved words of 'Mothering Sunday'. It would make so many mothers even happier!

With all best wishes

Mrs S F

I particularly appreciated the sentiments of this final card and wrote a suitable response. We do have many cards bearing the words 'Mothering Sunday', but being limited as to how many cards we can send out to the troops, her son must have received one of the more 'Americanised' versions!

Sticking with a patriotic theme, I have already mentioned my involvement with The Royal Society of St George, and I am proud to provide the flowers – red roses of course – for the Mansion House Banquet, and for the St George's Day Dinner at the Guildhall.

THINK OF A CARD...

A mate of mine from The Royal Society of St George is Don Coombe. He is a South London lad made good and we have known each other for years. Don established a charity called The Pelican Trust to help children from difficult backgrounds and I am pleased that *Clinton Cards* has been able to help him in some small way in this great work.

Then there is our involvement with The Duke of Edinburgh Awards, a fantastic scheme from which over 750,000 young people have benefited since its inception in 1956. With a presence in well over 100 countries, the aim is to reach the million mark by the end of the decade. As a company, our small part in this mammoth organisation is to support the Silver Award, something we are very proud to do as it is so inspiring to see the youth of today engaged in such wholesome activities.

It is always difficult to decide which charities to support and, conversely, which to decline, but there is not a bottomless pit so decisions always have to be made. My private charities have no part in this book, but as a company charitable giving has to be declared in our annual accounts and so I am happy for names to be included. We seek to ring the changes every year, and whilst we would always like to do more we have to be realists. As we are a quoted company, we have to produce profits for our shareholders – if we didn't *Clinton Cards plc* would suffer and so, inevitably, would the charities we support.

Over the years we have supported a wide range of charities, including the Winged Fellowship Trust, the Cheshire Homes, the Royal Star and Garter Homes and the Helen Rollason Heal Cancer Charity, among others. Helen Rollason was such an inspiring lady and it's so appropriate that an award has been established in her honour which is presented on the *Sports Personality of the Year* programme watched by millions.

In 2007 our selected charities included Barnardo's, the British Heart Foundation, the RSPCA, Marie Curie Cancer Care, and GUCH. The latter is the Grown Up Congenital Heart Patients Association and, like many people, we only got involved when the charity became personal. My son Clinton had a good friend who suffered from a heart defect and who, tragically, died as a result. During the course of Robert Bennett's illness, Clinton learned a lot about the excellent work of the charity, and decided it was one we had to support. I have learned through the charity that over 150,000 adults in England and Wales have been born with a heart disease and that over half will experience medical or social problems at some time in their adult life.

Despite ringing the changes, there are some organisations, like the Royal British Legion, which remain constant in our affections. We have introduced a range of cards with pictures of poppies on them, the entire proceeds of which go towards the work of this most worthwhile cause.

Another personal association has been with the Guide Dogs for the Blind, and for some time I was able to support the training of three dogs a year. I even had the honour of naming them... although I'm not sure how my son felt about his canine namesake!

Another favourite is the Essex Wildlife Trust, and for those of you who have no knowledge of Essex, no, this in not a contradiction! Regrettably, Essex has had a less than complimentary press from certain sectors of the media over recent years, something wholly unjustified and only perpetuated by those with little knowledge of this great county. I'd better get down off my soapbox again! To help educate some of you, Essex boasts 87 nature reserves, managing 7,200 acres, and *Clinton Cards* is proud to be a Corporate Member.

A large part of the work of the Essex Wildlife Trust is to educate, especially the young, which is another subject close to my heart. Indeed, *Clinton Cards* has been involved with West Hatch High School in Chigwell for some years now, and I was given the honour of opening a new state-of-the-art business and enterprise centre in February 2003. The school was only one of 18 in the country to have been granted such specialist status the previous year. As with the Duke of Edinburgh Award Scheme, it is great to see young people helping themselves, and it's encouraging to see so many bright youngsters around.

Despite having to draw a line somewhere – after all, there is the little matter of running a business as well – perseverance does pay off, as it did for two ladies who came to see me about a breast cancer charity. Despite my being busy, they would not take no for an answer and eventually got in to see me. I was so impressed by their enthusiasm that I agreed to sell a teddy in our shops for cancer awareness. Well done, ladies!

Another rewarding charitable venture was when we teamed up with the greeting card publisher *Andrew Brownsword*. We had been involved with the 'Forever Friends' bears since their creation by the illustrator Deborah Jones for the Andrew Brownsword Collection in 1987. These bears had captured the hearts of many of our customers, so when it came to the tenth anniversary of Forever

Friends, *Clinton Cards* and *Andrew Brownsword* were happy to donate 5p for every card sold. In this way we were able to buy three Sunshine Coaches for the Variety Club of Great Britain.

* * *

I suppose a chapter about charities would not be complete without reference to the thorny issue of charity cards, about which, you will not be surprised to learn, I have some pretty strong views.

I have always been sceptical about the business of charity Christmas cards, as some retailers see it as a marketing opportunity rather than having any serious desire to make a difference. Rather than raise my blood pressure by spouting forth, I'll leave it to one of the many articles I've read over the years. This one is from the *Evening Standard* of 23rd November 2001.

Choose your Cards with Care

Millions of us get a warm glow from buying charity Christmas cards each year, but an *Evening Standard* survey has found that many of these so-called charity cards give as little as 2p in the pound to good causes.

Clinton Cards, which gives 21% to four charities including Barnado's and Marie Curie Cancer Care, and *Paperchase*, which donates between 16 and 20% depending on the pack, are among the best on the high street.

"I don't see why, if *Clinton Cards* can offer 21%, other retailers can't follow suit," says Hilary Blume of the Charities Advisory Trust which advises charities on trading issues. "You couldn't put 2% meat in a pie and get away with calling it a meat pie."

Sadly, the picture was no better four years later, when *The Daily Mail* printed its own list of High Street Scrooges.

Liberty	5%
Harrods	6%
WH Smith	8%
Fenwick	8%
Dickens & Jones	8%
John Lewis	8%
Selfridges	9%
Next	9%
Cards Galore	9%
Waterstones	10%
Marks and Spencer	10%
Boots	10%
Paperchase	14%
Clinton Cards	21%

Don hadn't reported his missing credit card, simply because whoever had stolen it was spending *far* less than his Wife.

10 | Towards the Millennium

If any business is to survive the cut and thrust of the commercial world, it cannot stand still. Having reached 30 years in the business I might have tried to give the impression of sitting back and enjoying what had been achieved so far, but in reality I was looking to the next big challenge. This arose when I heard that the *Greetings Store Group (GSG Holdings)* was planning a flotation.

The directors of *GSG* were astute businessmen, having grown the company rapidly in four years, almost exclusively through acquisition. However, they were not 'greetings card' men. Their hearts were not in the card business – they were just out to grow a business and in this they had done very well. My hunch was that such people are often happy if they see a good return, as they are not usually in the industry for the love of it. They make their money and then look for other opportunities in other industries... or retire and enjoy the fruits of their labours.

I suppose I'm of the old school. I believe passionately in greeting cards. I have lived and breathed them for most of my life and so no one can accuse me of looking to make a quick buck and then retire. Retire... what's that?

A few phone calls would resolve my hunch, and, indeed, within days we had started negotiations. These came to fruition five months later in September 1998. The article in *Retailer* appeared before we were ready to make a formal announcement to the City, but by then the deal had been struck and it was just a matter of the legal boys dotting the 'I's and crossing the 'T's.

The Magnificent 700
Don Lewin, Chairman of Clinton Cards, seems a very happy and relaxed man.

His happiness is easy to understand, his relaxed state is less so. In one £27.5 million swoop he looks set to head up the world's largest specialist card retail chain. The acquisition of 211 shops from the *Greetings Store Group* will mean that *Clinton Cards* will swell to over 700 branches and command a 16% market share.

The proposed acquisition was well received in the City especially as it was announced alongside *Clinton Cards'* improved interim results. However, something the City analysts will not concern themselves with are the other reasons why *Clinton Cards* has made a bid for *GSG*.

Don Lewin leads from the front. He is a card man through and through and still spends every Saturday visiting what he refers to as "my shops". Expanding further he said, "It is important for me to see things as the customers see them." He sees it almost as a personal failing that there are "around 200 of our shops I have not visited recently." Don now has another 211 shops to add to his Saturday shopping list.

Don is justifiably proud of how his business has grown and the benefits its growth has brought to the industry.

"I look around the trade and I realise that so many publishers would not be here today were it not for *Clinton Cards* and that makes me feel good. As I have pointed out to publishers over the years, without *Clinton Cards* many would have a stack of cards sitting in their warehouses. We are their passage to the consumer and I feel proud that our hard work has paid off and made *Clinton Cards* the leading greeting card chain in the world" – and why Don Lewin now has the letters OBE after his name!

As rags to riches stories go, Don Lewin's is a good one. The son of a chimney sweep, he has pursued his entrepreneurial talents, remained firm in his business ethics and has sought to build-up the greeting card industry including pioneering new occasions such as St George's Day.

But the *Clinton Cards* story has not finished yet, and neither has Don Lewin's place as its leader. There are another 20 *Clinton Cards* shops due to open by Christmas, and Don still feels sure that there is room in the marketplace for 1,000 *Clinton Cards* shops, and then of course there is always the possibility of overseas expansion. Just think of

Don's Saturday shopping schedule then, but this does not faze him.

"While they did a good job, the *GSG* directors were only in it for the short term, looking to make some money and then move on. There is nothing wrong with that, if that is what you want to do. It's just that I'm in it for the long haul," he says as if his 30 years since *Clinton Cards'* conception is just for starters.

As if to highlight this point Don, with a glint in his eye said, "I see Irving Stone [head of *American Greetings*] as a role model. He is 84, is still really sharp, goes into the office every day and sees every piece of artwork, so I have a good few years to go yet!"

* * *

This acquisition helped us notch up two more milestones along the way: our selling space passing the one million square feet mark, and our first shop overseas… well, Northern Ireland to be precise. With most of these new shops in Scotland and the north of England, I would have plenty of travelling to do now on my Saturday morning jaunts… and I'd better invest in some anti sea-sickness pills too!

One of the advantages of buying *GSG* was that they had already dipped their toe in the water of EPOS (electronic point of sale) systems, something we had been looking into for some time. For all its considerable merits, problems associated with computer technology are legion. It seems incredible that what sounds like a simple concept in broad terms, for example introducing a stock control system or word processing package for head office, suddenly becomes fraught with problems when it comes to implementation. In my experience, whatever price the computer salesman quotes for a new computer system can be doubled or even trebled by the time all the glitches have been resolved at the exorbitant day-rates they like to charge.

Don't get me wrong, I am a fan of technology when it performs a valid function, and computers have helped to make us extremely efficient in reducing mountains of paper and analysing which shops are performing best and which require some assistance. But over the years I have learnt from all this and I am happy to let others become the trailblazers. Sticking to the technology maxim, 'the leading edge is the bleeding edge', I prefer to wait until systems are proven and robust before investing my hard-earned cash. Consequently, we were able to learn from GSG's initial forays into the world of EPOS, building on their good work as we looked to roll it out across all our shops.

EPOS enabled us to scan all products, so we could see at a glance which lines sold well. We had already introduced our own data warehousing system to help with stock control and re-ordering, so by marrying the two systems together we were provided with numerous dimensions with which to view group or individual shop sales. However, despite this potential plethora of information, I was keen that the figures would not rule us. I have always worked on gut instinct, which is why I like to visit all of our shops from time to time. Nothing beats that personal touch, walking into a shop, getting a feel for it, meeting the staff and chatting to customers.

By this time electronic systems were also in place with most of our suppliers, making the whole supply chain faster and more efficient. This may all sound easy, so I will not disillusion you by detailing the dozens of frustrating board meetings discussing technology – it was always the item I dreaded most on the agenda!

Moving towards the new millennium we also decided to indulge in that other technical necessity, national TV advertising. For the first time we ran a two-week campaign prior to Christmas, which was followed by a week of advertising leading up to Valentine's Day and again for Mother's Day.

All this technology would not have been complete without expansion onto the internet. Our website became operational in December 1999, starting in quite a modest way, but today I find it amazing. In addition to all the usual details about how to order and delivery services, there is useful advice about job and career opportunities, financial information for would-be investors and a store locator to find our nearest shop. There is also a calendar, which can be personalised for birthdays, anniversaries and other significant dates. The customer is then emailed in advance to ensure those special dates are never forgotten... I wonder if this was designed with men in mind!

When it comes to what we now offer, I am almost blown away. In addition to a vast array of cards and gifts, wedding paraphernalia, party packs and invitations, most of which can be personalised, we also offer a large selection of beautiful flower arrangements, with courier delivery, along with chocolates, champagne and our famous cuddly toys.

However, it is the gift ideas which I find incredible. These can be of the gentle and sophisticated variety like tea for two at *Harrods* or pampering at a top health spa, a night at the theatre or a trip to watch whales and dolphins at sea. For the adrenalin junkies we offer bungee jumping and skydiving... both of which can be done indoors or out!

When it comes to driving experiences, everything is offered from *Ferraris* and *Lamborghinis* around the Silverstone Grand Prix track, to tanks and monster trucks over rough terrain. Flying includes hot air balloons, microlights and *Tiger Moths*, and under sport and leisure you can learn to dance, taste wine or have a tour around a stadium like Twickenham, Old Trafford, Stamford Bridge or Anfield. Almost unbelievably, there is also a section called 'Wet N Wild', which offers white water rafting, driving speedboats or sailing a tall ship... and there was me thinking I ran a card shop! Whatever would Abba and Maurice have thought!

I was also soon to find myself in the catering business, but nothing that would worry Jamie Oliver or Gordon Ramsay. Our small offering was a coffee shop incorporated into our new store in Bath. By relocating two stores we were able to open our largest shop to date: 10,500 sq ft of selling space... including a coffee shop!

This shop allowed us to display the most comprehensive selection of our range, even when devoting space to seasonal products. It was wonderful to see such an amazing selection, and to realise how far the industry had come since I opened that single shop in Epping. It was truly breathtaking.

THINK OF A CARD...

A further initiative was with concessions in department stores. In November 1999 we tried out four concessions in *Debenhams*, and as they worked well we proceeded with dozens more the following year.

I got a warm feeling one weekend when I was reading the *Sunday Express* and the name 'Clintons' jumped out at me from the sports pages. The report of the Aston Villa Liverpool match was harping on about an apparently trigger-happy referee and included the sentence: "If he likes cards so much, why not spend his Saturday afternoons working behind the counter at *Clintons*?" It's one thing the City quoting impressive figures right, left and centre, but it's even more satisfying when the popular press can refer to us in such familiar terms.

Whilst talking about warm feelings, this is as good a time as any to write about one of the proudest days of my life. I might be proud about my business, but that's as nothing when it comes to my family, as any dad will know.

When Clinton married Julie in 1994 he asked George Darlington to be his best man. George had always been round our house as a nipper, but it was while he was sitting at the top table at Clinton and Julie's wedding that I appreciated how he had grown into a really impressive young man. I was obviously not the only one to have noticed George that day, because he started appearing at our house more regularly. By this time, of course, Clinton had left home, and George was certainly not there to visit Rose or me. His attentions were directed towards Debbie, who seemed equally keen to develop the friendship.

Then one day George did come round to see me. Despite him being a director of the family firm, *Darlington Motors*, I suspected that he had come to talk to me about something far more important than cars. He very politely and respectfully informed me that he would like to marry Debbie and he asked for my approval. Rose and I were obviously delighted by the prospect, but it was only afterwards, over a glass of champagne that he told me how terrified he had been about approaching me!

Debbie and George set a date for July 1999, and by virtue of my OBE they were entitled to marry in St Paul's Cathedral. Well, this was an opportunity not to be missed, especially as Clinton was too quick off the mark to be able to use the same venue. He should have had more confidence in his old man and waited!

Then came the question: "Where should we hold the reception?" There were plenty of suggestions convenient to St Paul's Cathedral, but I was delighted when Debbie said that she'd like the reception held in our back garden. Rose was over the moon too as she and Debbie could really go to town now. The ideas were not slow in coming, but at least our house in Chigwell was fairly new and so did not need a lot of attention.

It was decided to have a marquee in the garden and we also booked the Ray McVay Orchestra for the occasion. I have always been a fan of big bands, and what better excuse than my own daughter's wedding. We used external caterers who did a splendid job, and thankfully there was no irritating 'Fronk' figure, familiar to anyone who has seen the film 'Father of the Bride' with Steve Martin.

THINK OF A CARD...

As I say, it was one of the proudest days of my life walking Debbie down the aisle in St Paul's Cathedral, then welcoming the new Mr and Mrs Darlington into our home in Chigwell. As we walked through the living room out to the marquee in the garden with the orchestra playing, I was the proudest man in England. The day was made all the more special because Clinton was best man... a truly wonderful occasion.

As if a wedding was not enough for one year (and working at *Clintons* of course!), Debbie decided that she needed an extra challenge, so she ran the London marathon in April. When interviewed afterwards she claimed that, "being a director at *Clintons* is harder work than running the London marathon." I couldn't possibly comment. Debbie did amazingly well, clocking up a very creditable 4 hours 50 minutes and raising £15,000 for Age Concern in the process. In fact I was so impressed I allowed her a lie-in the following morning to help her get over her aches and pains. I told her that I didn't mind if she was ten minutes late into the office... just on this one occasion mind!

Whilst writing about the family, this seems an appropriate place to include more about Clinton. In October 1999 I was interviewed by *The Independent* newspaper about how we had worked together for over 20 years and this is what appeared:

> It was Clinton's headmaster who told me he wanted to join the business. I wanted him to work for someone else and learn a bit more from others, but he was adamant. He came in on the understanding that he'd start as a shop assistant

and work his way up. I'd done every job in the business so it was important Clinton did the same.

It wasn't until he reached 20 and thought he knew it all that we started to have the odd conflict. He'd have these great ideas, like home-brand cards, but unfortunately I'd already tried them and they hadn't worked. Once you put your name on something and you can't sell it, you're stuck. Timing is everything in this business, particularly if a product is tuned to a film release. We had a disastrous time with the film *ET* because all the merchandise, like the *ET* toys, arrived too late.

One of our biggest successes was being first with the Teletubbies. One lady was so desperate to buy a Tubby, she charged in before the shutters were up and cut her head.

Clinton certainly has a flair for the products. He's been selecting cards since he was 14, so I know his choices are good. He understands the real nuts and bolts are in the sentiment or what I call the 'Ah' factor. We don't always agree on things, but that's true of any partnership. The main difference with having your son as your partner is that you can't sack him. He tends to run before he's walked, whereas I like to take more time over decisions, which comes from age and hard-earned experience.

At times he can be a bit over-zealous, although he's growing less so as he gets older. He's a lot like me, which is one of the reasons we have our differences.

I spend Saturdays going round the stores, but these days I don't get around as much as Clinton.

He's doing the jobs I used to do, selecting the products and choosing the sites. Getting the sites right is one of the most important jobs and it's often a source of disagreement. When I first opened in Oxford Street everyone thought I was mad. Nobody had put a card shop on three floors before, yet it's been really successful. The only problem with the larger store is the level of security you need. When I started it never occurred to me that anyone would want to pinch a card. These days they take the entire rack. It amazes me how anyone can walk out of a shop with 300 cards, but they do.

I'm extremely fortunate Clinton joined me. I know a lot of successful guys whose sons don't want to know, but Clinton is passionate about the business. He leads from the front and puts in a hell of a lot of hours. Sometimes I phone him and he's in Scotland and the next day in Devon. When he's working in the office I know he's the first to arrive and is here long after everyone else has left. He's totally dedicated, which is why the staff have a lot of respect for him. I named the business after him, and the staff do call him Mr Clinton. I'm a cowboy fan, so he's named after Clint Walker. I think it's an asset that everywhere Clinton goes his name is up in lights.

In a way I'm glad he didn't have to experience the kind of hunger that drove me. I know a lot of my ambition to succeed came from growing up when times were tough. I was chopping wood and selling coal at the age of nine, doing anything to make money.

I remember being so ambitious I could almost taste it. Clinton and I share the same ambition for the company, in that we want to make it profitable. Sometimes he's more extravagant and wants to put more into a shop than I think is necessary. At those times I like to think he listens to my advice, although I don't know whether he accepts it. I certainly don't need to advise him as much because he's a grown man and knows what he's doing.

I've never doubted his talent. He's got a real sense of humour, a terrific personality and he's well liked. He's got it all, which makes me very proud.

I know there will come a time when Clinton takes over, but it's not in the foreseeable future. Retirement kills off people like me. I'd just vegetate. I enjoy being chairman; I'm the one dealing with the problems no one else can handle. I'm always looking two years ahead and for new ideas to move us forward. Ambition is about wanting something that is out of reach. I still have goals. We could double our size to 1,400 shops and be in every town, like *Boots*.

I started with nothing so it's been a hard slog. Sometimes I hear people say they started with nothing when I happen to know their parents had money to help them. There was none of that with me; I really did start from the ground up, which is quite an achievement.

* * *

Having had so much to celebrate of late, it seemed a shame not to complete the year on a high, and what better than the opening of our new flagship store in Oxford Street, the world's largest card shop. Initially on two storeys, the shop opposite Bond Street tube station had scope for a further floor in due course. At 4,500 sq ft per floor, it was vast and boasted escalators, and solid oak balustrades on the stairwells. The large front window was dominated by two water feature displays, so it was only fitting that Charlie Dimmock, of BBC TV's *Ground Force* programme, famous for her water features (among other things!) popped along to help with the opening. As Stuart Houlston, our property director, had personally overseen the project and headed the team, it was only fitting that he cut the official ribbon.

A few interesting facts were compiled by Stuart during construction of this giant store:

Over 2,500 McMuffins and bacon sandwiches were consumed;

Over 10,000 cups of coffee were drunk;

Over 7,000 hours of sleep were lost;

Over 45 tonnes of steel and 35 tonnes of screed were needed.

All in all it added up to a phenomenal building, almost beyond my wildest dreams… and it boasted over 5,000 different card designs. If you can't find what you want among that lot, all I can say is that you are hard to please!

So as the new millennium drew near I was able to look back with some satisfaction. We had celebrated 30 years in the industry with the major acquisition of *GSG*. This had brought us to over 700 shops, plus a number of smaller concessions, in the process raising staff numbers to 6,000.

In addition to all this, the website was up and running and we were confident of our computer systems surviving the dreaded 'Y2K' bug which so many doom-mongers predicted would bring an end to the technological world as we knew it.

Even the City seemed to like us, profits having doubled to £15.8m in the 1998 year-end results. The first half of 1999 even turned in a profit for the first time in ten years, thanks to help in the plush department from the US TV cartoon characters, *South Park*. As this is traditionally the quiet time of the year, the share price responded accordingly, hovering around the 300p mark. Everything in the garden looked rosy.

More importantly, the family was all settled and healthy, and so it was just a matter of looking towards the new millennium to see what challenges it might bring.

Congratulations On The
Birthdays Acquisition!
November 2004.

As a Christmas present for Mr Don Lewin OBE, all the Directors chipped in so he could buy a couple more shops!

11 | Going Shopping

After the dizzy heights of 1999, the New Year brought us crashing down to earth with a bump. Talk about the morning after the Lord Mayor's show!

Sales for October and November (ironically precisely the time when our share price was at its peak of 319p) were down 4.8% from the previous year. This necessitated a profits warning, and with it the share price fell by one third! The price had already fallen to 233½p and this tumble of 71p in one day took it to 162½p. Ouch! It continued to fall and even a 4.2% rise in profits for the year, bringing with it a record £17.6m, only produced a rally of 16p.

Whilst such figures are not enjoyable, I had learned well before now not to let my actions be driven by share price fluctuations – rise or fall. I know the card industry better than anyone and I also know that what we do, we do well, so it was just a case of nose to the grindstone and continue with the hard graft.

Thankfully August brought forth a great cause for celebration. The fourth of the month saw Queen Elizabeth, the Queen Mother's 100th birthday. I was not going to miss the birthday of all birthdays, and commissioned a specially made card, which I signed and sent, along with tens of thousands from other loyal well-wishers, no doubt. The great lady had served us well throughout her life, especially during the difficult war years when she refused to leave the side of her husband and her country in our hour of need.

Over the next year or two the share price yo-yoed up and down and there were dozens of articles advocating *Clinton Cards* as a good share to buy. These coincided with strong results, but, as I said, I just kept my eye on the ball, doing what came naturally, and that was selling cards.

During this time Debbie was also invited to join the board. This may have been met with a mixed reaction in the City, but she has proved herself time and time again, having worked her way up from the bottom. Since her days as junior secretary and receptionist she had worked in personnel, but she really found her niche in product development. If anything, it was a lot tougher for Debbie because she had a certain surname to overcome. Anyone in the company with the name Lewin is going to find it difficult to live up to... perhaps that's why my brother Alan is known as 'Mr Alan' to staff and suppliers alike!

I was delighted that Debbie achieved her position on merit, not least because she finds it much easier to shoot from the hip than some other people I've come across. Being self-made, a few people have found me intimidating. I like to think that I am not and will listen to anyone with an opinion they can back up. I can take criticism – it's just that I don't suffer fools gladly. Debbie is nobody's fool and has never been afraid to speak her mind, a quality I admire.

It gives me a warm glow whenever I appear in surveys like the top 100 entrepreneurs in the country, and it was an especial honour to be named the *Ernst and Young* London Entrepreneur of the Year in 2002, co-sponsored as it was by the London Stock Exchange and *The Times*.

However, what gave me greater satisfaction was to see our Loughton head office on the Bond Street slot of the Essex Edition of *Monopoly*. This told me that *Clinton Cards* had made its way into the heart of the local community, especially as 20,000 people had voted to name the various segments. My only real concern was the price of the site: £1,400 with a hotel on it... I hope no one snaps it up too soon!

* * *

As part of our ongoing search for new business opportunities, we trialled 35 temporary seasonal Calendar Experience sites in 2001. These worked well and by 2002 a further 93 sites had been added. Additionally, in November 2001 we opened a 'megastore' and the new 'largest card shop in the world' with our 10,500 sq ft store in Bath. Following on from the success of this we identified 50 further sites for these megastores... with coffee shops, of course.

We also like to run competitions from time to time, both as a bit of fun and as a way of generating some publicity. These might be of a local nature and we are keen to support our shop managers in such initiatives. On a national scale, in the year 2000, to tie in with Father's Day, we ran a competition to find the UK father most like Homer Simpson, arguably the world's best known dad.

The Simpsons was a huge hit in the United States and the UK at the time, and Homer was the focus – that loving devoted dad with strong family values, often undermined by his all-too-human failings. Our judges were looking for dads who not only bore a physical resemblance to the cartoon character (not necessarily a desirable quality!), but who also shared his characteristic parenting skills.

The prize was pretty special, a trip to *The Simpsons Fanfest*, a worldwide celebration of 'All Things Simpsons' in Hollywood to commemorate ten years of *The Simpsons* on TV. There were also prizes of official *Simpsons* merchandise for the runners-up.

The following year, in our 'Red Card' competition we were looking for dads with a devotion to the family and a passion for football. Unsurprisingly, there was no shortage of entrants as the prize was not to watch any old match, but to go to the Nou Camp to watch the mighty Barcelona.

Another popular initiative was the Nurse of the Year competition we ran in conjunction with Marie Curie to help celebrate that most deserving of professions. Tied in with Nurse's Day, the idea was to help Marie Curie raise the profile of their Cancer Care home nursing service, hospices and research work.

I pride myself in having done just about every job in the company. This was certainly true in the early days, but now I would be struggling to keep up with all the clever technology-based jobs that are so necessary, like keeping all our computers and communications running and dealing with the internet etc.

I like to be in the office by 9 o'clock, so I swim every morning between 6.00 and 7.00 as it keeps me fit as well as giving me a chance to collect my thoughts for the day ahead. Whilst I have an indoor swimming pool at home, I find the atmosphere more congenial at the local leisure centre so I swim there instead. Some of the regulars have sussed out who I am, but I like to keep a low profile – after all, having made a bit of money does not make me anybody special. However, this can create the odd awkward moment, like when a chap asked what I did for a living. I replied, quite truthfully, "I work for *Clinton Cards*."

I learned to be a little more discreet after having a massage on one particular occasion. Being an East End lad, it took me many years before I felt comfortable going to health clubs and having a massage, but I was introduced to *Champneys* by my friend Harry Dupay and I found it to be most agreeable. However, even then it took a few more visits before I would venture into the strange world of having a massage. Actually, I was pleasantly surprised by how relaxing it was and I was soon chatting quite contentedly to the masseuse. He knew of my connection with *Clinton Cards* and said something about the share price going up. This was soon after the company had been floated and it had been a good period for us, so I mentioned that it had made me a couple of million quid. This was my mistake. I felt his fingers stiffen in my back and I received a much more rigorous massage than planned!

Another of my passions is singing and I love the sort of music favoured by the likes of Frank Sinatra and Dean Martin. I like to think I have quite a good voice, although others might not necessarily agree. Naturally, given my line of work, I send personalised Christmas cards, and for the past few years this has been a musical card with me singing my Christmas wishes. Last year it was a variation of the 1920s Walter Donaldson and Gus Kahn number, 'Making Whoopee'. It was originally sung by Eddie Cantor, although Ray Charles had a much bigger hit with it in the 1960s. Since then it has been covered by any number of singers, but I am sure none have treated it quite so casually. I changed the words to, 'Make me Happy', and with my love of writing verse I scribed an appropriate review of our year. I'm not sure how well it was received, but I hope it brought a smile to a few faces... and I haven't heard of any cancelled contracts.

THINK OF A CARD...

With profits going in the right direction, we planned an expansion programme having now fully integrated all the *GSG* shops into the *Clinton Cards* portfolio. There were hopes of 800 shops by 2006, with the magical 1,000 figure being achieved by 2010. Part of the plan was to significantly increase the number of outlets in Scotland from 50 shops, and also to build on our success with the larger stores.

This sort of organic growth has always been at the core of my business philosophy, unless, of course, other opportunities arise in the meantime which are too good to ignore, as had happened with the likes of *Hallmark, Carlton Cards* and *GSG*.

A competitor I had been keeping my eye on for some years was Ron Wood and his company *Birthdays*. Our paths rarely crossed in the early years, because *Birthdays* was based in Lancashire, but by the early 1990s they boasted a very respectable 200 shops, 45 of them being franchise operations. It was at this stage that Bryan Robson, the Manchester United and England captain had a stake in the business.

By 2002 I was aware that the *Birthdays Group* might be open to an offer, and, indeed, in April of that year it was reported in the press that we were interested and that talks were talking place. We were interested, as I had been for several years, but only if the price was right. There is no sense in growing for growth's sake – it has to be at the right price.

It transpired that we were not the only interested party. The Scottish entrepreneur Tom Hunter had made his money with the *Sports Division* retail chain, selling it to *JJB Sports* in 1998 for £290 million, making him Scotland's richest man. He teamed up with another Scottish entrepreneur, Chris Gorman who made his millions during the internet boom and who held a £15m share of *The Gadget Shop* retail chain. It was reported that the intention was to combine *Birthdays* with *The Gadget Shop...* an interesting concept!

Tom Hunter and Chris Gorman called their company *West Coast Capital*, buying the *Birthdays Group* for a reported £60m. This was well above what I valued the business to be worth – even with 450 shops in the portfolio – so I was happy to stand by and watch what they could make of it. They would be better men than me if they could turn in a profit on what they had paid, but only time would tell.

The waiting game paid off. Only a year after buying the *Birthdays Group*, Messrs Hunter and Gorman got in touch for a chat. Like the astute businessmen they are, they rapidly assessed the company and rather than throw good money after bad they decided it was time to call it a day.

Many column inches appeared about the new acquisition, but because I was personally interviewed for the article, I'll leave the analysis to the industry magazine, *Progressive Greetings Worldwide*.

Worℒh the Wait

It took four attempts for *Clinton Cards* to acquire *Birthdays*, but it has been worth the wait for the Loughton-based group. Not only is the £46.4 million deal considerably lower than its last bid, but a lot of the 'sorting out' of the *Birthdays'* business has been done by previous owners, *West Coast Capital*.

THINK OF A CARD...

Progressive Greetings catches up with Don Lewin, chairman of the now enlarged *Clinton Cards* group, to find out what it feels like to be selling Christmas cards from over 1,250 shops this year.

"Buying *Birthdays* is the easy bit. We've now got to make it work," Don Lewin, chairman of *Clinton Cards* comments to *Progressive Greetings* shortly after the announcement was made last month that, subject to shareholder approval on December 6, *Clinton Cards* has acquired *Birthdays*.

Don Lewin is very upfront as to his intentions of keeping *Birthdays* as a stand-alone business "to capitalise on the strength of the *Birthdays* brand name... I don't want to bury *Birthdays*, I want to make it work," stated Don.

Don gives over an air of being fairly relaxed on the supplier score. "There is room for everyone," he says enthusiastically.

A similar enthusiasm sweeps away any suggestion of Don retiring. With 1,200 stores now on the company's books, has he not surpassed his self-imposed goal of running 1,000 shops before retirement?

"I meant 1,000 *Clinton Cards* shops – so we still have 200 to go on that count. And I might like to have 1,000 *Birthdays* shops too!"

The final word must rest with the ultimate authority, the *Financial Times*, which paid us the compliment of writing a greeting card-style verse to mark the occasion:

> Put out the flags! Shout hip hooray
> For this is *Clinton's* special day.
> Congratulations, high street vendor
> Of cards; I wouldn't want to be the sender,
> With verse so mawkish, trite and maudlin',
> They make this doggerel sound like Auden.
>
> Yet with your special retail art,
> You've won a place in many a heart,
> And now you've topped it with a meal:
> You're buying *Birthdays Group*, a deal
> That's costing 40 million smackers;
> A price that doesn't seem too crackers.
>
> The analysts, 'tis true, are sniffy,
> They wonder if the strategy's iffy.
> Your business is mature, they say,
> And buying earnings a short-term stay.
> But you have synergy gains to reap...
> The shares are up; so don't lose sleep.
>
> Congrats then, on this special day,
> You dreamed – and did it your own way.

12 | To the Future…

Integrating hundreds of new shops into the *Clinton Cards* fold has been a stimulating exercise over the past three or four years. We have had to decide which shops have the best location and most potential, inevitably having to close some where the proximity is not right. An exciting part of an amalgamation is getting to know the new staff, the lifeblood of any organisation, especially one so dependent on dealing with the public. We now have many thousands of staff, and almost without exception I can say that I am mightily impressed by everyone who works for us.

The favourite part of my job over the years has always been visiting our shops on my Saturday morning jaunts, or just when I happen to be in a different part of the country for one reason or other. I love it, especially when I haven't played any part in the design or even the location of the shop, which has happened more often in recent years, particularly as we have acquired a number of shops from other companies. Firstly, I usually have a look from the outside, getting a feel for the high street or shopping mall, drinking in my first impression of the shop, because first impressions are so important as far as customers are concerned.

I then usually wander into the shop and just look round like any other customer. I have a somewhat critical eye, but here again I am usually delighted by what I see. I might make a mental note or two, but they are usually only minor details.

Sometimes I might be recognised by the manager or one of the staff, especially if word has spread from local branches that I am in the area. I prefer it if I am not recognised because I can then see how everything runs normally, without the staff feeling they are on show, so to speak. I love it when there is a general feeling of friendliness in the shop, as is usually the case, the staff clearly enjoying their work and interaction with customers.

First impressions are important, but I learnt a sobering lesson many years ago when I arrived early in a shopping mall and so had a cup of coffee in a nearby cafe until the shop opened. I started to feel frustrated as the time drew near to 9 o'clock, yet still there was no sign of any staff. At about 8.50 a flamboyant platinum blonde tottered along on her stilettos, clearly in a bit of a rush. I thought to myself that she was cutting it fine, and if I am honest I was not too impressed by her appearance or her time-keeping. However, I kept my distance, waiting for opening time.

Just before 9 o'clock the shop opened, the other staff had arrived and they were ready for business. I had a look around, loved what I saw and was most impressed by how the staff interacted with the early customers. When I eventually introduced myself to the manager, it was clear that she knew the business and her clientele thoroughly, that she loved her work and that she was highly professional in all respects. It made me feel embarrassed that I had had initial misgivings.

I often remind people at head office that it is the thousands of full-time and part-time staff who work in the shops who make

Clinton Cards the great company it is, and that they are the ones who pay all our wages. The most important part of any company is its customers, consequently any staff with direct contact play a vital role.

I must take this opportunity to record my thanks to all those who have worked for *Clinton Cards* over the years. I know I expect a lot, but there have been countless occasions when even I have been amazed at the hours people have put in, especially during the time of the flotation and the rights issue. I might be daft enough to work every hour under the sun, but there again *Clinton Cards* is still my baby. For other people to choose to do so voluntarily is most humbling – thank you all.

It is always invidious to pick out just a few people to thank personally, but there's little alternative if this book is not to look like a telephone directory, so here goes.

When we started thinking about a quotation on the Unlisted Securities Market it became obvious that we needed help from a major accountancy firm, which is how I got to know Robert Gunlack, a partner with *Price Waterhouse*. Robert advised that we needed to appoint a high calibre accountant internally and said that in Barry Hartog he had just the man for me. However, by this time I was well advanced in discussions with Simon Layer, who was a similar age to Clinton and clearly a man with a bright future. I employed Simon, who did a wonderful job getting us through the minefield of the USM quotation. However, with this sizeable achievement under his belt, Simon was soon looking for bigger and better opportunities in the world of high finance and so left with our blessing. It was then that Robert advised that Barry Hartog might still be interested. Barry had worked for *WH Smith*, being made managing director of the newly acquired *Our Price* records chain. Within 20 minutes of meeting Barry I knew he was the man for us, as indeed he has proved time and time again. I can honestly say that I have enjoyed working with Barry every day he has been with us.

I have been extremely lucky in attracting many of the big names in the card industry over the years, one of whom was George Pomphrett. George was at the opening of our 50th shop, which was in Southend. He was managing director of *Celebration Art Group* (*CAG*) at the time, one of our major suppliers. I took to George – after all, he was a good East End boy who liked his pie 'n' mash. In chatting, I learned that he was after the top job at *Carlton Cards*. George just missed out on this, instead being put in charge of European operations. Going to Paris once a week might sound glamorous, but the novelty soon wore off and so when I phoned him for a chat he was open to my suggestion of becoming our operations director. I could probably have tempted George earlier, but I felt it was important for him to see if he could get the top job at *Carlton Cards* first. I would have hated him coming to us regretting that he hadn't given it a shot, always wondering 'what if?' As it was, George was delighted to join us, becoming a stalwart of *Clinton Cards* for many years.

John Robinson came to us from *Superdrug* when he was in his late twenties. I liked his ambition and so was happy to take him on as a senior regional manager. Since 1988 he has done a variety of jobs, growing with the company. Having put up with me for 20 years he is now buying and marketing director, so he can't be such a bad lad.

As I've said before, I admire anyone who is not frightened of hard work. That work ethic matched with ability means that you can go far in *Clinton Cards*. This has certainly proved to be the case for Ivan Crow who joined as a shop manager in Chelmsford in 1984. He is now our card buying director, having come up through the ranks of area and regional manager before joining us at head office. Seeing talent blossom in this way, as I've also observed with hundreds of our shop managers, gives me just as much pleasure as seeing the business grow – indeed, without such talent, it couldn't grow.

Our director in charge of general buying, Brett Smith, also started as a shop manager, although for him *Clinton Cards* was already in the blood as his father Don was an area manager. Brett was not even 20 when he took charge of his own shop in Peterborough before starting his meteoric rise. Life has not even begun for him at 40, yet he is already a director, having spent half his life with *Clinton Cards*.

Like Stuart Houlston, managing director of *Birthdays*, Mike Bugler learned the card business with *Hallmark*, a company I admired for their professionalism. Mike joined us as director of buying, but took over as managing director of *Clinton Cards* when Clinton assumed overall responsibility for both companies.

Other top people to have joined us from the premier league of the card industry over the years, and without mention of whom this book would not be complete, include Peter Osman, Stuart McKay,

THINK OF A CARD...

Ray Cousins and Brian Jackson. All of them have done sterling work to help make *Clinton Cards* the success story it is today.

Another couple of stalwarts who have clocked up nearly 60 years between them are Alice Wiltshire and Rita Rawlings. They were both at the old 'head office', a room above a shop in Chingford. Doris was the third member of the team; she was the book-keeper. When Doris eventually retired we had a little celebration for her and I marked the occasion with a special card... at least she thought it was special until she read the back. It said, "Not for Resale!" giving everyone a good laugh. Since moving to Loughton, Rita has become Clinton's PA while Alice runs customer services.

There are others who also warrant a mention. It was whilst we were living in Epping that Mrs Greaves first came to do some cleaning for us. Rose was pregnant with Debbie at the time and needed help. Interestingly, she worked for us at every subsequent house we've lived in over the past 40 years. She even came to clean the silver after she retired... and I still called her Mrs Greaves right up until the day she died.

As the size of our gardens increased I advertised for a new gardener, which was when Tony came to see me. I was surprised when he said that he could only offer me three days a week because I had specifically advertised for a full-time gardener. He was working two days for Billy Smart, yet Tony seemed to think that three days would be sufficient to deal with what I wanted. There was something about the chap I liked so I was happy to listen to him. He ended up by saying, "Give me a try and see what you think – after all, you've got nothing to lose." I had to admit that he had a point, because if he could do what I wanted in less time, then I was quids in. Tony was as good as he claimed and he has been with me ever since – that's at least 30 years now – although he has subsequently come on board full-time.

Then there is Melvin who has been with me for 27 years. Initially he started as an odd job/handyman working in a small company with his uncle, but since then Melvin has turned his hand to most things: electrics, carpentry, plumbing, building work – you name it he can do it, and he's so professional.

As the company started to grow to a significant size, it made sense to employ a chauffeur so that my time could be used more profitably in the car, reading reports and making phone calls. Garry has been my chauffeur for years, having the knack of knowing when I fancy a chat and when I've got other things on my mind. Obviously, when there are other people in the car I have to sit in the back, but sometimes when it's just the two of us and I've done my work, I'll sit in the front with Garry. I feel more comfortable that way rather than trying to be someone I am not.

This reminds me of a conversation I had with a chap who had done very well for himself, but boy did he know it. He was one of those I mentioned earlier who had had a helping hand in life, being born with a silver spoon in his mouth. We were at a hotel when he asked me why I bothered to chat to waiters and cleaners. Initially I couldn't understand what he was getting at; I have always chatted to everyone, no matter who they are or what they do – I've got time for anyone who works hard and tries to make an honest living. I must admit, my opinion of this chap dropped dramatically… which is why I'm not giving him the satisfaction of seeing his name in my book!

Other people who have proved invaluable over the years have been Mike and Paula. Mike is our warehouse manager. He is one of those people who can turn his hand to anything, and Paula is similarly versatile; her primary job is cleaning at head office, but she's also happy to help out elsewhere when needed. The pair of them will do anything for me.

Again, thank you all.

* * *

So now *Clinton Cards* has reached the momentous milestone of 40 years. Wow! I wonder what the next 40 might bring? That won't be for me to decide as I will have passed the baton on long before then, but quite when remains to be seen. As long as I continue to have the same passion for my work and feel that I can make a significant contribution, I'll still be at my desk.

I have had a wonderful roller-coaster ride over the past 40 years. I have met some amazing people and feel hugely proud that our small offering makes such a difference to so many people's lives. It has been a privilege, so thank you all.

To close I would like to include the verse I scribed for one of Rose's recent birthdays... it's never wise to divulge a lady's age.

Dearest Rose

This is a special card
Especially made for you,
To make the day you have chosen,
To have a party, too.

Two hundred plus will be there
To say, "Have a real grand day,"
While I sit in the corner
Saying, "Who else do I pay?"

It will be a day to remember,
If I have got it right.
We start in the early evening
And go on till late at night.

I know you will enjoy it all,
There's sober and there's funny,
But just don't make it every year,
'Cos I don't have that much money.

It now remains for me to say,
Happy Birthday to you, the other half,
And if this verse was any good,
It should have made you laugh.

As you can see, I like writing a bit of poetry, but I think I'd better leave it to the professionals as far as the cards in our shops are concerned!

Appendices

Appendix 1 – Top Business Tips

Appendix 2 – Facts and Figures

Appendix 3 – My First Academic Qualification

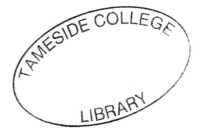

| My Top Tips for Success

Here is a list of my tips for success I came across recently. They were printed in the City section of *The Sun* newspaper, so they must be true.

1. If you want to achieve something you have to be ambitious enough to work at it night and day.

2. Remember where your roots are and keep your feet on the ground no matter how successful you become.

3. Always be ready to listen to others and learn from them. Adapting to new ideas is a must.

4. Keep in touch with your workers and your products. Visit your branches as often as you possibly can.

5. Every business needs the support of a good bank, accountant and lawyer.

6. If you want respect you have to earn it. Always do exactly what you say you are going to do and say what you mean.

7. A sense of humour is always a great asset.

8. Earn the loyalty of employees by being loyal to them.

9. It's important to keep motivated. I get up early every day to swim and keep fit.

10. Remember that as you build the business you are building a future for your family and future generations.

A Few Facts and Figures

The first commercial Christmas card was 'invented' in 1843 by Henry Cole, founder of the Victoria and Albert Museum. It was designed by his friend John Calcott Horsley (brother-in-law of Isambard Kingdom Brunel). One thousand copies were printed, selling for one shilling each.

One of Sir Henry's first Christmas cards, sent to his grandmother, was recently sold at auction for £22,500.

The 'Henries', the annual greeting card industry awards, are named after Sir Henry Cole.

The UK greeting card industry is worth over £1.5 billion annually – more than the combined markets for tea and coffee.

This comprises three types of buying:

> 60% Everyday – birthday, get well, anniversary etc.
> 30% Christmas
> 10% Spring – Valentine's Day, Mother's Day, Easter,
> Father's Day

THINK OF A CARD...

The UK boasts the most successful greeting card industry in the world with 800 publishers producing over 2.87 billion greeting cards in 2006.

5,500 cards are sold every minute, and if all the cards were placed end to end they would stretch around the world more than 17 times!

More cards are sent per capita in the UK than anywhere else in the world:

> 55 UK
> 48 USA
> 38 Canada
> 30 Australia
> 30 Scandinavia
> 25 Netherlands

In 2007 The *Clinton Cards Group*:

Operated from 1,075 shops, with 1,872,000 sq ft of selling space

Employed 8,845 staff, rising to over 10,000 at Christmas

Sold 176,861,366 cards

Sold 13,234 miles of giftwrap... that's more than halfway round the world!

Generated in excess of £500,000,000.00

Vice-Chancellor
Professor Martin Everett BSc MSc DPhil AcSS

UEL
University of
East London
www.uel.ac.uk

Don Lewin
Chief Executive Officer
Clinton Cards
The Crystal Building
Langston Road
Loughton
Essex
IGN 3TH

12 May 2008

Honorary Doctor of Business Administration
Each year the University of East London offers a number of honorary awards to celebrate the lifetime achievements of individuals who have made a distinguished contribution to their field of endeavour. We make the awards at one of our graduation ceremonies hoping that the achievements of those receiving our honorary awards will inspire our graduating students in their future lives.

In recognition of your own work, I am delighted to write to ask you to accept the award of the Honorary Doctor of Business Administration of the University of East London. The award would be conferred by our Chancellor, the Lord Rix, at our awards ceremony to be held at the Barbican Centre on 26th November 2008. We have coffee at 10.15 a.m. and the ceremony itself starts at 11.00 a.m. After the ceremony the Chancellor hosts a lunch for the honorary graduates and the event draws to a close around 2.15 p.m.

I would be grateful if you would contact me at your earliest convenience and at the latest by 6th June, to let me know if you will be able to accept this invitation. If so, I will confirm the further details of the arrangements nearer the time.

I look forward to hearing from you and very much hope to have the pleasure of your company later in the year

Martin

Professor Martin Everett
Vice-Chancellor

Docklands Campus, University Way, London E16 2RD
tel: +44 (0)20 8223 4000   fax: +44 (0)20 8223 4100
e-mail: m.everett@uel.ac.uk   web: www.uel.ac.uk

CUSTOMER SERVICE EXCELLENCE   INVESTOR IN PEOPLE

The University of East London has campuses at London Docklands and Stratford
If you have any special access or communication requirements for your visit, please let us know. MINICOM 020 8223 2853